A THEORY OF INTERPRETATION OF THE EUROPEAN CONVENTION ON HUMAN RIGHTS

A Theory of
Interpretation of the
European Convention
on Human Rights

GEORGE LETSAS

OXFORD
UNIVERSITY PRESS

OXFORD

UNIVERSITY PRESS

Great Clarendon Street, Oxford OX2 6DP

Oxford University Press is a department of the University of Oxford.
It furthers the University's objective of excellence in research, scholarship,
and education by publishing worldwide in

Oxford New York

Auckland Cape Town Dar es Salaam Hong Kong Karachi
Kuala Lumpur Madrid Melbourne Mexico City Nairobi
New Delhi Shanghai Taipei Toronto

With offices in

Argentina Austria Brazil Chile Czech Republic France Greece
Guatemala Hungary Italy Japan Poland Portugal Singapore
South Korea Switzerland Thailand Turkey Ukraine Vietnam

Oxford is a registered trade mark of Oxford University Press
in the UK and in certain other countries

Published in the United States
by Oxford University Press Inc., New York

© G. Letsas, 2007

The moral rights of the author have been asserted

Crown copyright material is reproduced under Class Licence
Number C01P0000148 with the permission of OPSI
and the Queen's Printer for Scotland

Database right Oxford University Press (maker)

First published 2007

All rights reserved. No part of this publication may be reproduced,
stored in a retrieval system, or transmitted, in any form or by any means,
without the prior permission in writing of Oxford University Press,
or as expressly permitted by law, or under terms agreed with the appropriate
reprographics rights organization. Enquiries concerning reproduction
outside the scope of the above should be sent to the Rights Department,
Oxford University Press, at the address above

You must not circulate this book in any other binding or cover
and you must impose the same condition on any acquirer

British Library Cataloguing in Publication Data

Data available

Library of Congress Cataloging in Publication Data

Letsas, George.
A theory of interpretation of the European Convention on Human
Rights / George Letsas.
  p. cm.
ISBN 978-0-19-920343-7
1. Convention for the Protection of Human Rights and Fundamental
Freedoms (1950) 2. Human rights—Europe—Interpretation and
construction. I. Title.
KJC5132.L485 2007
341.4′8—dc22   2007035284

Typeset by Newgen Imaging Systems (P) Ltd., Chennai, India
Printed in Great Britain
on acid-free paper by
Biddles Ltd, King's Lynn, Norfolk

ISBN 978–0–19–920343–7 (Hbk.)

1 3 5 7 9 10 8 6 4 2

To my parents

Acknowledgements

In Woody Allen's *Annie Hall*, the camera pans around a Hollywood Christmas party when one of the guests, dressed in a pretentious space costume, is overheard saying: 'Right now it's only a notion but I think I can get the money to make it into a concept and later turn it into an idea'. This book has been through all three of these stages; it started as a vague and fuzzy notion in the form of a PhD proposal in 2000, was made into an interesting concept upon succesful completion of a doctoral thesis in 2005, and was finally turned into what I hope is a clear idea in 2007.

I am deeply grateful to my two thesis supervisors (now colleagues) at UCL, Stephen Guest and Ronald Dworkin, for the time they devoted to my work as well as for their invaluable feedback, support, and encouragement while writing the thesis. I should mention that attending the UCL Colloquium in Social and Political Philosophy chaired by Ronald Dworkin has been the best philosophical training one could ever hope for. I owe Ronald Dworkin a great debt for inspiring a love for normative jurisprudence and political philosophy. I have also benefited enormously from the UCL Jurisprudence Discussion Group and the Pre-Colloquium in Social and Political Philosophy organized and chaired by Stephen Guest. My grateful appreciation to Stephen Guest who has been enormously generous with his time, guidance, and indispensable support.

No amount of reading is a substitute for philosophical conversation. Most of the ideas in this book were formulated after long, day-to-day, Socratic-style conversations with friends and colleagues to whom I am deeply grateful: Octavio Ferraz, Nicholas Hatzis, Peter Jaffey, Dimitris Kyritsis, Stuart Lakin, Virginia Mantouvalou, Saladin Meckled-Garcia, Riz Mokal, Carlos Perez-Vasquez, Eva Pils, Nicos Stavropoulos, Stavros Tsakyrakis, Dimitris Tsarapatsanis, and Emmanuel Voyiakis. They not only endured these long conversations (some of which were alcohol-free) but also read and commented on early drafts. Special thanks are also owed to Colm O'Cinneide, Sean Coyle, Aileen Kavanagh, Jamie Meyerfeld, Eric Barendt, and Dawn Oliver for their comments on specific chapters of the book. I am particularly grateful to Matthew Craven and Zenon Bankowski for their valuable comments and in-depth criticisms of my doctoral thesis. I would also like to thank Nicos Alivizatos, Dawn Oliver, Constantinos Papageorgiou, Vassilis Voutsakis, Ralph Wilde, and Jonathan Wolff for the support and inspiration that they have provided over the years. A special mention must be given to Virginia

Mantouvalou whose constant support and constructive criticism have been extremely productive but whom I failed remarkably to convince about the soundness of the main arguments in this book.

I benefited enormously from the comments of the anonymous reviewers for the Press which helped me to clarify many points, shift the focus where necessary, and sharpen the arguments advanced in the book. Many thanks are also owed to the anonymous reviewers of the *European Journal of International Law* for their in-depth criticisms and comments on an earlier version of Chapter 2 which was published in 2004. An earlier version of Chapter 4 (Two Concepts of the Margin of Appreciation) was published in the *Oxford Journal of Legal Studies* in 2006. I also presented some of the ideas in this work in staff seminars held in the Law Department of the University of Leicester in March 2007 and at UCL in January 2006, November 2006, and January 2007. Many thanks to all participants for their helpful comments and criticism.

While writing the thesis I received financial support from the Greek State Scholarships Foundation (IKY), as scholar in Philosophy of Law (by examination). I would like to thank the supervisor of the scholarship in Greece, Professor Pavlos Sourlas for his constant support and kindness, as well as express my gratitude for everything that I have learned from him. The award of the *Georg Schwarzenberger Prize in International Law* by the Institute of Advanced Legal Studies (IALS) was a great honour and motivation in writing up my thesis.

I would like to thank John Louth, Rebecca Smith, and Lucy Stevenson of Oxford University Press for their patience and professionalism. I am particularly grateful to Rebecca Smith for taking the book through the various stages of approval and final submission in the most kind and patient way.

Last and most certainly not least, very special thanks are due to my family and friends for their love, patience, and support.

Contents—Summary

Contents

Table of Cases

Table of Legislation

Introduction

Do Europeans have a right to have an abortion? A right to publish cartoons that offend religious people? A right to assisted suicide and euthanasia? A right publicly to deny the holocaust? These are important moral and political questions. But they are also important legal questions whose answer depends on the rights that the European Convention on Human Rights (ECHR) grants to the 800 million people that live in Europe today. Yet the text of the Convention is not clear about whether Europeans do have these rights and many other rights even more controversial. Nor do officials, lawyers, and judges agree on what rights the law of the ECHR grants. Does it follow that no such legal rights exist? How are we to tell?

The ECHR was drafted within the Council of Europe, a political organization founded in the aftermath of the Second World War in order to defend democracy, the rule of law, and human rights in Europe. The Convention is now more than 50 years old.[1] Since 1998, the European Court of Human Rights (ECtHR) has had exclusive jurisdiction to receive individual applications. The recognition of the right to individual application before the Court is compulsory for all Member States and the judgments of the ECtHR are binding.[2] In international human rights law, the European system is considered to be a model of effectiveness.[3] Its success is manifested in many ways, both in the effect it has had on domestic law[4] and in the increasing number of applications being lodged before the ECtHR that has over the years generated a rich and extensive human rights case law, unique in international law. Rolv Ryssdall, one of the Court's former presidents, described the ECtHR as 'a quasi-constitutional court for the whole of Europe'.[5]

In the last 10 years, however, the effectiveness of the European system has been under threat from two directions. First, the Court became a 'victim of its

---

[1] It opened for signature in Rome on 4 November 1950 and entered into force in September 1953.

[2] On the reform of the system by the 11th Protocol see, Drzemczewski A, 'The European Human Rights Convention: Protocol No. 11—Entry Into Force and First Year of Application' 21 *Human Rights Law Journal* (2000) 1.

[3] See Ryssdall R, 'The Coming of Age of the European Convention of Human Rights' 18 *European Human Rights Law Review* (1996) 18.

[4] See Bernhard R, 'The convention and domestic law' in Macdonald R, Matscher F, and Petzold H (eds) *The European System for the Protection of Human Rights* (1993) 25.

[5] Ryssdall R, 'The Coming of Age of the European Convention of Human Rights' 22.

own success',[6] having difficulty managing the ever-increasing caseload.[7] This is partly to do with the increased awareness of the right to individual application within Contracting States and partly with the enlargement to Eastern Europe, following the collapse of the Eastern bloc. Membership doubled within 14 years, from 23 in 1990, to 46 in 2004.[8] Secondly, the enlargement to Eastern Europe raised questions about the human rights records of the new Member States and the Court's prospects of applying the same human rights standards to cases coming from the new members as those developed for the older western European ones.[9]

These developments only added to problems that the ECtHR was already facing in interpreting the ECHR. By looking at the relevant literature and the case law, one finds a series of important jurisprudential issues that have been raised in relation to the interpretation of the ECHR. One way or another, these issues point to the relationship between the two foundational principles of a supranational human rights system: state sovereignty on one hand and the universality of human rights on the other.

There are three more specific issues that triggered my investigation into the interpretation of the ECHR and form the subject matter of this book. The first is the worry that the judges of the European Court of Human Rights will exercise illegitimate judicial discretion if they interpret the Convention in a creative way. The second issue is the controversy over the interpretive methods actually used by the Court, in particular, the charge that these methods are not being applied with clarity or consistency or that they are in themselves objectionable. The third and final issue has to do with the moral foundations of human rights more generally and the extent to which the Court's interpretation of the Convention rights conforms or should conform to them. Let me discuss these three issues in turn.

The literature on the interpretation of the ECHR is dominated by a general hostility towards judicial creativity on the part of the European Court of

---

[6] See Dembour MB, '"Finishing Off" Cases: The Radical Solution to the Problem of the Expanding ECtHR Caseload' 5 *European Human Rights Law Review* (2002) 604.

[7] To solve the problem of the caseload, the system is currently under reform by Protocol 14, which opened for ratification in May 2004. One of the most controversial provisions in Protocol 14 is the introduction of a new admissibility criterion. According to the amended art 35 ECHR an application will be inadmissible 'if the applicant has not suffered a significant disadvantage'.

[8] These are: Albania, Andorra, Armenia, Austria, Azerbaijan, Belgium, Bosnia and Herzegovina, Bulgaria, Croatia, Cyprus, Czech Republic, Denmark, Estonia, Finland, France, Georgia, Germany, Greece, Hungary, Iceland, Ireland, Italy, Latvia, Liechtenstein, Lithuania, Luxembourg, Malta, Moldova, Monaco, Netherlands, Norway, Poland, Portugal, Romania, Russia, San Marino, Serbia and Montenegro, Slovakia, Slovenia, Spain, Sweden, Switzerland, Turkey, Ukraine, United Kingdom, and the former Yugoslav Republic of Macedonia.

[9] See Leuprecht P, 'Innovations in the European System of Human Rights Protection: Is Enlargement Compatible with Reinforcement?' 8 *Transnational Law and Contemporary Problems* (1998) 313.

Human Rights. The source of this hostility is not always clear. Some take vagueness or uncertainty to be an inherent feature of legal rules that gives judges an illegitimate power of discretion, which must be restrained. This is the line taken by Paul Mahoney, the former registrar of the European Court, who has written extensively on the interpretation of the ECHR. Mahoney argues that, 'the open textured language and the structure of the Convention leave the Court significant opportunities for choice in interpretation; and in exercising that choice, particularly when faced with changed circumstances and attitudes in society, the Court makes new law'.[10] Other commentators follow the same line. Matthijs de Blois, in an essay on the 'fundamental freedom' of the European Court argues that, 'most substantive provisions of the Convention leave much room for different interpretations. They are therefore a source of judicial discretion'.[11] Others have claimed that the Court should take into account the intentions of the drafters of the ECHR. Lawrence Helfer argues that Strasbourg organs 'risk judicial illegitimacy whenever they depart from an interpretation based on the intent of the Convention's drafters'.[12] Similar concerns have been raised by judges of the ECtHR.[13]

What all these views share is the idea that creative interpretation marks a case for illegitimate judicial discretion. These commentators complain not only that Strasbourg organs go beyond pre-existing law whenever they exercise choice in interpretation but also that by doing so they act illegitimately and should therefore show some restraint. The idea that choice in interpretation amounts, by default, to illegitimate discretion is used to wave the flag of judicial self-restraint.

The second recurrent theme in the literature on the interpretation of the ECHR is the inconsistency or lack of clarity in the methods used by the Court, most notably the margin of appreciation doctrine. Lord Lester criticized the Court's use of the doctrine as being 'slippery and elusive as an eel'.[14] Others have complained that very often the Court's use of the doctrine masks the real basis for its decision.[15] In reading the Court's judgments, one often forms the

---

[10] Mahoney P, 'Marvellous Richness of Diversity or Invidious Cultural Relativism' 19 *Human Rights Law Journal* (1998) 2. See also Mahoney P, 'Judicial Activism and Judicial Self-Restraint in the European Court of Human Rights: two sides of the same coin' 11 *Human Rights Law Journal* (1990) 57: '"Judicial activism" in the sense of making new law is therefore inevitable'.

[11] de Blois M, 'The Fundamental Freedom of the European Court of Human Rights' in Lawson R, de Blois M (eds) *The Dynamics of the Protection of Human Rights in Europe* (1994) 51. See also Ost F, 'The Original Canons of Interpretation of the European Court on Human Rights' in Delmas-Marty M (ed) *The European Convention for the Protection of Human Rights* (1991) 238.

[12] Helfer L, 'Consensus, Coherence and The European Convention on Human Rights' 26 *Cornell International Law Journal* (1993) 135.

[13] Cf the dissenting Opinion of Judge Matscher, *Öztürk v Germany* (1984) Series A no 73.

[14] Lord Lester of Herne Hill, 'Universality Versus Subsidiarity: A Reply' 1 *European Human Rights Law Review* (1998) 73, at 75.

[15] See Macdonald R, 'The Margin of Appreciation' in Macdonald R, Matscher F, and Petzold H. (eds) *The European System for the Protection of Human Rights* (1993) 85; Singh R, 'Is there a role for

impression that the doctrine of the margin of appreciation is a device used to defer to the judgment of national authorities, particularly when the legal issue before the Court is politically sensitive and there is likely to be significant political opposition by the respondent state to the Court declaring a violation.

The third and final issue arising in the context of the interpretation of the ECHR is an increasing controversy regarding the nature and scope of the rights embodied in the Convention. The cases that have come before the European Court of Human Rights in recent years pose serious interpretive challenges. Does the right to life under art 2 ECHR include the right of a terminally ill patient to terminate her life?[16] Does the right to private life under art 8 ECHR include the right to sleep at night free from airplane noise?[17] Does the right to property under art 1 Protocol 1 ECHR entitle the former King of Greece to claim compensation for the expropriation of royal property following a referendum on the abolition of the monarchy?[18]

These interpretive challenges are followed by another trend in the practice of the ECHR which I call the inflation of rights. It is argued that the protection of the ECHR should be extended to new areas such as armed conflict and humanitarian intervention,[19] social rights,[20] and labour rights.[21] Do these areas fall within the scope of the rights embodied in the ECHR? Even if they did not initially, should perhaps the Court 'read them' into the Convention now?

Some may think that the above questions and the normative issues they raise are purely academic because judges will decide cases according to their own political views, or because the way the ECHR is interpreted is bound to reflect a political compromise between various competing interests. This is not the approach taken in this book. How law should be interpreted, and what legal rights individuals have, is taken to be an important question of political morality that is both capable and in need of principled justification. Judges have a responsibility to justify their decision and cite the reasons that led them to it. In doing so they cannot help but engage, either directly or indirectly, with the above normative questions. This should be even more so in the case of the

---

the "Margin of Appreciation" in national law after the Human Rights Act?' 1 *European Human Rights Law Review* (1999) 15.

[16] *Pretty v United Kingdom*, Judgment of 29 April 2002, Reports 2002-III.

[17] *Hatton v United Kingdom* (Chamber), Judgment of 2 October 2001; *Hatton v United Kingdom* (Grand Chamber), Judgment of 8 July 2003.

[18] *Former King of Greece v Greece*, Judgment of 23 November 2000, Reports 2000-XII.

[19] See *Bankovic and Others v Belgium and Others*, Judgment of 12 December 2001, Reports 2001-XI.

[20] See Cassese A, 'Can the Notion of Inhuman and Degrading Treatment be Applied to Socioeconomic Conditions?' 2 *European Journal of International Law* (1991) 141.

[21] See Ewing KD, 'The Implications of Wilson and Palmer' 32 *Industrial Law Journal* (2003) 1.

ECHR, a human rights instrument that has brought together all European states and has an important effect on both domestic law and culture.

The issues I referred to above (ie judicial discretion, legitimacy, interpretation, and philosophy of rights) have occupied a dominant place within Anglo-American legal, moral, and political philosophy for the last 40 years or so. Following the publication of John Rawls's *A Theory of Justice* in 1971, Anglo-American philosophy has witnessed an unprecedented production of normative work in legal and political theory. This literature, and particularly Ronald Dworkin's and John Rawls's work, has been a real inspiration for this study. One of the aims of this book is to introduce discussions within Anglo-American normative legal and political philosophy to the interpretation of the ECHR. As far as I know, there have been very few such jurisprudential approaches to the ECHR.[22] On the contrary it has been suggested that Anglo-American legal theory is ill-suited for the ECHR.[23]

In this book I argue that the ECHR enshrines human rights that are both *legal* and *liberal*: they entail liberal egalitarian principles that impose conditions on the legitimate use of coercion by Member States against persons within their jurisdiction. Legality and liberalism are objective values of political morality that should shape and guide the interpretation of the ECHR. They impose two very important requirements. First, that the benefit of the moral principles which justify the ECHR rights should be extended equally to all Europeans. Secondly, that the ECHR rights should give effect to people's responsibility for choosing and pursuing their own conception of the good life and protect them against moralistic and paternalistic restrictions on liberty. The value of the ECHR rights does not consist in securing that individuals will live a better or a good life, or that their well-being will be improved. Part of the book is devoted to criticizing areas of the European Court's case law that violate these two requirements.

These requirements might sound foreign to many European ears and be seen as an uncritical import of American ideology which may not travel well in Europe. The institutional role that religion plays in Christian Europe and the commitment to a welfare state in many European states, are but a few

---

[22] Two exceptions are Nowlin C, 'The Protection of Morals Under the European Convention for the Protection of Human Rights and Fundamental Freedoms' 24 *Human Rights Quarterly* (2002) 264 and McHarg A, 'Reconciling Human Rights and Public Interest: Conceptual Problems and Doctrinal Uncertainty in the Jurisprudence of the European Court of Human Rights' 62 *Modern Law Review* (1999) 671. Steven Greer's 'Constitutionalizing Adjudication under the European Convention on Human Rights' 23 *Oxford Journal of Legal Studies* (2003) 405, is a very useful account of the Court's approach in every article but it does not address broader philosophical issues regarding judicial discretion and the moral foundations of human rights.

[23] This point is made in relation to Ronald Dworkin's legal philosophy by de Blois M, 'The Fundamental Freedom of the European Court of Human Rights', at 41.

examples where Europe differs significantly from the USA. Consider religion. Many human rights violations that the European Court has had to deal with over the years, like prohibition of homosexuality and obscene art or rights to abortion and euthanasia, are sensitive moral issues over the handling of which the church is taken to exercise a legitimate influence within many European states.[24] By contrast, US constitutionalism, for all its flaws, has consistently challenged the legitimacy of such an influence as a matter of principle, despite the fact that Americans are not less religious than Europeans. As to welfare policies, Western Europe has traditionally rejected the libertarian US model and insisted instead on a stronger welfare state and greater state regulation of the economy. Courts in Europe are often seen as deputy legislators who may legitimately promote and expand widely accepted social goals. It is therefore no surprise that the idea of social and economic human rights as well as the concept of positive obligations[25] are very popular in Europe but are met with scepticism in the US.

Yet despite these cultural and political differences, and many others which are beyond the scope of this book, the main questions that a human rights court, like the ECtHR, is facing are specific and common to all constitutional courts. This means that the answers cannot be culture-specific save for a reason which itself cannot be culture-specific. What moral rights individuals have by virtue of being human, and what institutional responsibility courts have when they apply the law, are not things we would normally expect to differ from country to country in the way taste in food and clothes do. Although I do not address meta-ethical issues of moral objectivity in this book, I believe, as most philosophers do, that wholesale sceptical attacks on moral truth cannot threaten our commitment to first-order moral beliefs of the kind that human rights express. As Donald Davidson puts it, the nature of belief is 'essentially veridical'[26] and 'all that counts as evidence or justification for a belief must come from the same totality of beliefs to which it belongs'.[27]

---

[24] See for example the case of *Otto-Preminger-Institut v Austria* (1995) 19 EHRR 34 and the relevant discussion in chs 5 and 7.

[25] On this concept see Mowbray A, *The Development of Positive Obligations Under the European Convention on Human Rights by the European Court of Human Rights* (Hart Publishing, 2004).

[26] 'Empirical Content' in Davidson D, *Subjective, Intersubjective, Objective* (2001), at 175. See also his groundbreaking masterpiece 'On the very idea of a conceptual scheme', reprinted in Davidson D, *Inquiries into Truth and Interpretation* (2nd edn., 2001) at 183.

[27] Davidson, D, *Subjective, Intersubjective, Objective* (2001) at 155. Davidson notes that anti-realist theories of truth make truth radically epistemic and face obvious counter-examples (each and every one of our beliefs may turn out to be false), whereas realist theories make truth radically non-epistemic and therefore potentially inaccessible. His solution is to view truth as a primitive concept which cannot be defined. See Davidson D, 'The folly of trying to define truth' 93 *Journal of Philosophy* (1996) 263. Davidson's theory differs from so-called

Moral scepticism makes a bad argument for cultural relativism about human rights[28] and the latter is almost always defended using communitarian, nationalist, anti-imperialist, or some other substantive argument. It therefore takes a moral reason, grounded on a universal value of political morality, to establish that the institutional responsibility of judges and the scope and foundation of human rights should be different in the case of the ECHR.

One such reason may stem from the obvious fact that the ECHR is not a constitutional document but an international treaty between sovereign states. I therefore begin in Chapter 1 by exploring whether international human rights differ from national human rights and whether international legality differs from legality in municipal law. Interestingly, Anglo-American liberal thinkers like John Rawls, Ronald Dworkin, and Bernard Williams have distinguished between international human rights and domestic constitutional rights along the lines that the former are fewer and more fundamental, a manifest assault on a basic notion of human dignity which is shared cross-culturally and need not rest on liberal principles.[29] International human rights organizations by contrast have tended to inflate the notion of human rights beyond the traditional list of rights found in the constitutions of western liberal democracies.

The argument advanced in this book, namely that the ECHR enshrines liberal rights, faces a double challenge. It must explain first why the ECHR rights should be given a liberal foundation which is politically parochial[30] and which widens the scope of the Convention rights beyond what can be agreed upon cross-culturally. But it must also explain why a liberal theory of the ECHR rights should be premised upon principles of anti-paternalism and anti-perfectionism and stop short of protecting welfare interests that are classified as human rights by international organizations (like the right to water, environment, work, health, and the like).

In Chapter 1, I address this challenge by drawing a distinction between different normative roles that human rights play. I argue that John Rawls's minimalist account of human rights in his *Law of Peoples* should not be seen

deflationist or disquotational theories of truth which argue that we can stop using the truth predicate altogether. See generally Horwich P, *Truth* (1991). Ronald Dworkin advances a type of redundancy or disquotational theory of truth in his 'Objectivity and Truth: You'd Better Believe it' 25 *Philosophy and Public Affairs* (Spring 1996) 87–139.

[28] See the discussion in Blackburn S, 'Relativism' in LaFollete H (ed) *The Blackwell Companion to Ethical Theory* (2000), at 38 and Waldron J, 'How to Argue for a Universal Claim' 30 *Columbia Human Rights Law Review* (1999), at 305–14.

[29] See the discussion in ch 1.

[30] Needless to say, it is politically parochial in the historical sense that it draws on liberal ideas developed in the Anglo-American world, from John Locke and John Stuart Mill to John Rawls and Ronald Dworkin. But these ideas are not parochial in their *justification* and *application* any more than Newton's law of gravitation is.

as offering an account of the rights that individuals have by virtue of being human nor of the moral foundations of rights found in existing human rights treaties. Rather, it is a theory that addresses a very specific normative question, namely: what are the conditions for tolerating non-liberal states and refraining from interfering with their domestic affairs? As such, it does not speak to the very different normative question, which the interpretation of the ECHR raises: what are the foundations of human rights found in legally binding international agreements? Unlike the United Nations human rights system, which promotes human rights in a politically diverse world, the ECHR has always been and still remains an agreement between European states to be legally bound by the values of liberal democracy.

A second distinction I draw is between human rights as acceptable political goals that international bodies may promote and human rights as legal rights. It seems to me that many international organizations, like the United Nations, use the vocabulary of human rights to express political goals that all states have a reason to promote: eradication of poverty, protection of the environment, reduction of corruption and unemployment, etc. Clearly the more these goals are served the better, from the point of view of the well-being of the affected individuals. But it does not follow that when these rights become legal rights, when, that is, they condition the way in which state coercion is used, they entail a legal obligation on the part of the state to maximize the value that these rights serve. This is not an argument about *which* rights can be justiciable but about the normative consequences of a right being justiciable. As Dworkin has argued, a state must govern through a set of coherent principles whose benefit it extends to all citizens.[31] Legal protection of human rights adds this very important dimension to their scope: no individual interest should be protected as a matter of human rights law unless it can be justified by a legal principle whose benefit is extended to all citizens. This creates a logical space between human rights as desirable political goals that may be promoted gradually and without necessarily using state coercion (eg through regulation, soft law, directives, etc) and human rights as *legal* rights which condition the legitimacy of state coercion. As a result, a lot of the work that governmental and non-governmental organizations do in identifying individual interests worthy of state protection (for example that noise pollution impairs the enjoyment of private life) need not be taken to be co-extensive with the homonymous right of the ECHR (eg right to private life). Human rights do set acceptable political goals to improve the welfare of individuals. But the *law* of human rights cannot aim to create obligations of outcome on the part of the state, ie obligations to ensure that everybody's

---

[31] Dworkin R, *Justice in Robes* (2006) at 13.

interests will be served up to a certain degree. In sum, there is, I believe, no *one-size-fits-all* theory of human rights either of their scope or of their moral foundations. When claiming a human right we must be careful to specify the normative context and the grounds on which it is claimed. If we care about the moral force and urgency of human rights then we must take great care not to turn everything into a human rights issue. We should not claim a human right first and ask questions about its moral foundations later.

Still, this argument from the value of legality faces considerable difficulty in the case of the ECHR. For the ECHR is an international law treaty, an agreement between sovereign states in a global order that lacks anything close to an international executive, legislature, or judiciary. As such, it is difficult to see how the ECHR rights can be governed by a value that conditions the legitimacy of the use of state coercion. Yet this objection can be met, I believe, in the case of the ECHR.[32] My main argument against this objection turns on the moral relevance of two characteristics of the ECHR. The first is that the ECHR is treated by the relevant actors (ie Member States, applicants, and judges) as enshrining rights that states have a *primary* obligation to respect when deploying coercive force, as opposed to a *secondary* obligation to compensate victims should they be found to be in breach of the Convention by the European Court of Human Rights. This attitude towards the ECHR is no less shared in Member States which follow dualism and in which domestic courts may not have jurisdiction to apply the Convention.

The second relevant characteristic of the ECHR is its subject matter: unlike international treaties on trade or commerce, the purpose of human rights treaties is precisely to prescribe what a state may not do to its own people. The right of individual application to the European Court of Human Rights and the fact that the judgments of the Court are binding would otherwise make little sense. The duties Member States undertake when joining the ECHR are primarily duties towards individuals within their jurisdiction as opposed to duties towards other Member States. The subsidiary character of the international protection of human rights, manifested in the requirement to exhaust domestic remedies, refers to a *procedural* question about the jurisdiction of courts, not to the *substantive* question of what legal duties Member States have. Controversial as it may sound, the book defends strongly the view that, as far as the nature and scope of human rights are concerned, the fact that the ECHR is an international treaty should make no difference.[33] Just

---

[32] I am more sceptical about the application of Dworkin's value of legality to other areas of international law, at least without any qualifications.

[33] This claim does not hold of course for the non-substantive provisions of the ECHR, such as art 1. Arguments for restrictive interpretation of such provisions on the grounds that the ECHR must be interpreted in line with the rest of international law of which it forms part, are in principle

like a constitutional court, the European Court has the final authority to rule on whether a state (through its statutory provisions, case law, or executive acts) violates abstract moral principles. What it rules on is inevitably an abstract issue of principle which it then must apply to all Europeans.

Since the early years of the European Court of Human Rights, substantive questions about the scope and limits of the Convention rights were bound up with considerations about the status of the ECHR as an international and subsidiary mechanism for the protection of human rights. In his dissent in the landmark *Golder* case, Sir Gerald Fitzmaurice argued that 'the parties cannot be expected to implement what would be an important international obligation when it is not defined sufficiently to enable them to know exactly what it involves'.[34] Judicial legislation, he argued, may be acceptable in domestic adjudication, but it is totally unacceptable in international adjudication which is based on agreement between states. The idea of ignoring drafters' original intentions, Fitzmaurice was urging in 1975, 'lacks realism and reason'.[35]

This and other calls for judicial restraint were largely motivated by concerns about the legitimacy and effectiveness of an international court whose powers were taken to depend exclusively on the will of Contracting States. Yet such calls ran against an equally strong tendency, particularly on the part of the applicants, to view the ECHR as granting rights that are independent of the will of the Contracting States. The case law on autonomous concepts which is discussed in Chapter 2 highlights cases in which the Court understood the ECHR rights in a non-conventionalist way: these rights need not be the same as those that the Contracting States (or the majorities in them) take them to be; rather, their basis is some substantive moral principle that justifies them and that calls for consistent application. As the European Commission put it as early as in 1968, 'If the Contracting Parties were able at their discretion to classify an offence as disciplinary instead of criminal ... the operation of the fundamental clauses of arts 6 and 7 would be subordinated to their sovereign will'.[36]

Chapter 2 concludes by arguing that in the face of disagreement over the principles that justify whether the applicant has a particular right under the

perfectly valid. This might explain why the European Court has been more cautious in cases like *Bankovic and Others v Belgium and Others*, Judgment of 12 December 2001, Reports 2001-XI and *Al-Adsani v United Kingdom* (2001) 34 EHRR 273 where issues of public international law arise. For a different view and related criticism, see Orakhelashvili A, 'Restrictive Interpretation of Human Rights Treaties in the Recent Jurisprudence of the European Court of Human Rights' 14(3) *European Journal of International Law* (2003) 529.

[34] Judge Sir Gerald Fitzmaurice, separate Opinion in *Golder v United Kingdom*, Judgment of 21 February 1975, Series A no 18, para 30.

[35] Separate Opinion in *National Union of Belgian Police v Belgium*, Judgment of 27 October 1975, para 7.

[36] *Twenty-One Detained Persons v Germany*, EComHR, Decision of 6 April 1968, Collection 27 (at 97–116), para 4.

ECHR, calls for judicial restraint beg the question. For it does not follow from the fact alone that applicants or states disagree about whether the ECHR grants a right that no such right exists. Human rights are not criterial concepts whose meaning is exhausted by their common usage across Contracting States. They are meant to express a moral commitment to objective principles of liberal democracy. It follows that the European Court of Human Rights does not exercise illegitimate judicial discretion in looking for and applying these principles to unforeseen and controversial cases.

Chapter 3 looks at the role that drafters' intentions and the text should play in the interpretation of the ECHR. The European Court has been relatively consistent in rejecting intentionalism and textualism as interpretive methods, in favour of the so-called 'evolutive' or 'living instrument' approach. The chapter provides a philosophical defence of the Court's approach drawing on the relevant debates about the interpretation of the US Constitution. Neither the text, nor drafters' intentions, can alone justify why the ECHR grants a particular right or not. Certainty and publicity, two values often cited in support of intentionalism and textualism, have no application in the ECHR which is neither meant to guide individuals' conduct nor to protect states' expectations about what their ECHR obligations are. On the contrary, the ECHR aims to prohibit states from treating individuals in a certain way, however convenient, natural, or justified states may find it.

The use of 'evolutive' or 'dynamic' interpretation may suggest that the Court rejects Member States' original intentions back in the 1950s only to endorse Member States' (or the majority of them) *current* intentions as to what is protected under the ECHR. After all, the drafting states now form a very small minority in the Council of Europe and it would be unfair to impose their interpretive intentions upon the current majority. The idea of current intentions, or current *consensus*, also figures in the case law on the margin of appreciation. Yet current consensus amongst Member States is as problematic as intentionalism and textualism. If the moral principles underlying the ECHR are independent of what most states thought, hoped, or expected back in the 1950s, then they are also independent of what most states think now. The same reason that justifies why drafters' intentions about the scope of the ECHR rights are irrelevant also justifies why current consensus is irrelevant. The only consensus that is morally significant is the one entailed by the drafting of the ECHR and the agreement to be legally bound by certain fundamental principles of liberal democracy.

The arguments in Chapters 1, 2, and 3 are largely negative in character. They locate the ECHR within broader philosophical discussions about human rights, international law, and legality, and argue that the ECHR legalizes liberal principles which impose normative conditions on the legitimate

use of state coercion, regardless of drafters' original intentions and Member
States' current consensus. They therefore advance primarily a theory of how
the ECHR should *not* be interpreted as opposed to a theory of how to interpret specific rights of the Convention or particular cases.

In Chapters 4, 5, and 6 I turn to the doctrine of the margin of appreciation
which has not been the best part of the European Court's case law. It is replete
with uncertainty and inconsistency. In an effort to address this controversy
I introduce, in Chapter 4, a distinction between two different uses of the doctrine in the case law. The first one, which I call the substantive use of the doctrine, refers to cases where the Court is invited to decide whether a particular
interference with a Convention right is justified in a democratic society under
the restriction clauses of the relevant articles of the ECHR, most notably arts
8–11 ECHR. The Court often uses the label of the margin of appreciation
to express a final conclusion as to whether a particular interference has been
justified without stating explicitly the substantive principle upon which that
conclusion is based. As such, the substantive use of the margin of appreciation
is redundant and the Court should stop referring to it and state instead the
principle justifying a particular judgment. By contrast, the second use of margin of appreciation, which I call the structural one, does express a substantive
principle of interpretation. It figures in cases where the Court believes it must
defer to the judgment of national authorities because there is no consensus
between Member States as to whether the applicant before the court has the
human rights he or she claims. The principle implied in these cases is that the
applicant does not have a right under the ECHR if there is not some consensus between Member States about the existence of this right or that the applicant's right consists solely in the treatment or the benefit upon which there is
consensus. In my view, this alleged principle should not be confused with the
notion of cultural relativism as it is motivated by beliefs about the appropriate
role of the European Court of Human Rights, not about the nature of rights.

Given the clear link between the substantive use of the margin of appreciation and the nature and moral foundations of particular rights, Chapter
5 looks at liberal theories of rights with a view to explain the idea that states
can justifiably interfere with Convention rights (under the relevant limitation
clauses). It also aims to provide, in a more positive way, a theory of interpretation of the ECHR drawing on fundamental liberal principles. The discussion
is structured around John Rawls's and Ronald Dworkin's work on the nature
of rights and the distinction between interest-based and reason-blocking theories of rights. I defend the claim that the ECHR does not create abstract
entitlements that certain individual interests be protected up to a certain
degree. It is misleading to think of justiciable human rights as rights to particular interests. Rather, we have rights not to be deprived of some liberty

or opportunity on the basis of certain impermissible considerations: that our plan of life is impoverished or immoral; that we are despised by the majority; that our views shock and offend others; that we should be forced to lead a particular kind of life; that our life is worth less than the life of others; that the majority will secure a marginal or speculative benefit by restricting important liberties. Rights thus understood are *absolute* and subject to no 'balancing' exercise: it can never become justified for the government to restrict someone's liberty on the impermissible considerations just mentioned.

Chapter 5 concludes with a list of liberal egalitarian principles of interpretation that aim to capture the anti-utilitarian, anti-perfectionist, and anti-paternalist character of rights. To be sure, these principles are not exhaustive of the normative content of the ECHR rights nor can they alone be used to justify other rights of the Convention, such as the right to property or the right to a fair trial. But whatever else the rights of the ECHR do, they should at least give effect to these liberal egalitarian principles. More specific principles figuring in the interpretation of other Convention rights must be consistent with and derivative of the anti-utilitarian and anti-perfectionist value of rights.

In the last chapter I return to the structural use of the margin of appreciation which I discuss critically in the light of the liberal egalitarian principles highlighted in Chapter 5. I look at three areas of the relevant case law. The first is cases in which the European Court has interpreted public morals as a justified ground for restricting rights, balancing the applicant's right against conventional morality. The second includes cases, like the British cases on transsexuals' rights and the Turkish case on the headscarves ban, where the Court has refrained from finding a violation on the grounds that the legal issue is either politically sensitive or there is no consensus amongst Contracting States about it. The third area refers to cases like *Hatton*, where the Court took protection of welfare interests, like the interest in sleep, to fall within the ambit of the ECHR, asking itself whether interference with these rights has been proportionate. I call this latter area an instance of 'inflation' of rights.

None of these three strands of the case law, under what I call the structural use of the margin of appreciation, can be justified under liberal democratic principles. For the use of consensus as an interpretative principle is bound either to give effect to the moralistic preferences of the majority or to authorize the use of state coercion in an unprincipled and arbitrary manner. Consider the case law on public morals. In one of the most famous quotes from its case law, the Court noted that freedom of expression is:

applicable not only to 'information' or 'ideas' that are favourably received or regarded as inoffensive or as a matter of indifference, but also to those that offend, shock or disturb the State or any sector of the population. Such are the demands of that pluralism, tolerance and broadmindedness without which there is no 'democratic society'.[37]

This passage has inspired generations of human rights lawyers and activists. Yet we should not forget what the Court also said in this judgment. It added that freedom of expression 'is subject to paragraph 2 of Article 10' which means that 'every "formality", "condition", "restriction" or "penalty" imposed in this sphere must be proportionate to the legitimate aim pursued'.[38] One of the aims stated in paragraph 2 is 'protection of public morals' and the European Court interprets this to include the right 'not to be insulted in [one's] religious feelings by the public expression of views of other persons',[39] moving on to apply a test of proportionality. Is this interpretation compatible with the demands of pluralism, tolerance, and broadmindedness, without which there is no 'democratic society'? How can one be said to have the right to offend, shock, or disturb when this right is subject to the rights of others not to be offended, shocked, or disturbed? Or is it that we have a right to shock and offend others, so long as we do not offend too much or we do not offend too many?

It is wrong to think that the limitation clauses of the ECHR open the door to an abstract balancing exercise between the various conflicting interests that are involved. The point of the limitation clauses is to invite the court to identify which principle justifies the right in question and to examine whether that principle applies to the applicant's case. For example, the value of democracy requires that we are free to express ideas and to try and convince others about their plausibility. This freedom is a necessary condition for the legitimacy of imposing the outcome of elections on individuals. This principle applies to religious speech as much as it does to political speech. It is therefore unprincipled to protect the expression of political ideas that shock or offend but censor speech which offends religious beliefs. In assessing whether a religious minority can advertise itself on the radio,[40] there is no 'margin of appreciation' to be taken into account and no balancing against the beliefs of the majority to be done. But the above principle does not apply to Holmes's example of falsely shouting fire in a crowded theatre: clear and present danger for the life of others is a legitimate reason for restricting speech.

Are liberal principles absolutely absolute, such that the European Court may never grant States a margin of appreciation on politically sensitive issues? It is often argued that the Court should allow a margin of appreciation to avoid frustrating states that are likely to withdraw from the Council

---

[37] *Handyside v United Kingdom* (1979–80) 1 EHRR 737, para 49.
[38] ibid.
[39] *Otto-Preminger-Institut v Austria* (1995) 19 EHRR 34, para 48.
[40] See the case of *Murphy v Ireland* (2004) 38 EHRR 212.

of Europe or to stop executing other judgments of the European Court that are less controversial. This argument is as valid in the case of the ECtHR as it is in the case of domestic constitutional courts whose judgments are also likely to frustrate the legislature or the executive in this way. Fifty years since the adoption of the ECHR, I doubt whether this likelihood is significantly higher in the case of the European Court than in the case of domestic constitutional courts, at least for the majority of Member States. Assessment of whether there is such clear and present danger should be done with caution, as the Court has done in certain cases.[41] Still, cases where such a danger exists are likely to be exceptional and rare.

Less exceptional and rare however have been cases where the Court reads various welfare interests into the ambit of substantive rights of the Convention, such as the right to private life, and then asks itself whether the interference with (or the failure to protect) that interest is justified or necessary. The best example of this trend is to be found in *Hatton*, where despite the fact that no violation was eventually declared, both the Chamber and the Grand Chamber took the interest to sleep well at night as falling within the protected scope of art 8. What is the principle however? As the applicants had the choice to move to a different area without any financial loss, I cannot think of a principle that can justify the claim that people have a legal right to sleep well at night.[42] It might be suggested that the interest to sleep well grounds a right because sleep is important no matter what one's plan of life is. But so is the interest to eat well, breathe clean air and have a decent income. If we have a right to sleep well under the ECHR (qualified as it may be) we also have a right under the ECHR to eat well, breathe clean air, watch good theatre and have a decent income. Principled consistency would require reading these rights into the ECHR too, inviting the European Court to decide when states have struck a fair balance. Such an inflation of rights would make it hard to justify why courts should institutionally have the last word on whether someone's rights have been violated.

There is more to be said about the interpretation of particular rights of the ECHR which this book does not address. The aim of this book is to discuss the most abstract and general issues that the interpretation of the ECHR raises, in the light of fundamental questions in moral and political philosophy.

The joke has it that an activist court is one whose judgments you disagree with. In this book I argue that the European Court has been hesitant in upholding liberal principles that I believe underlie human rights, whereas it

---

[41] See the discussion of the *Leyla Sahin* case in ch 6.

[42] The moral difference between the *Hatton* case and sleep deprivation as a form of torture is clear: the latter, but not the former, is an intentional infliction of pain by state officials on people who cannot escape it.

has shown willingness to protect interests that do not, in my view, fall within the institutional responsibilities of a human rights court. Am I simply refusing to accept that Europe has a different conception of rights, legality, and democracy, one that I happen to disagree with? Perhaps, but this does not show why this conception is the best one to have nor why we should keep it in the future. The claim that someone's human rights are violated is one of the most serious moral and political allegations, not to be taken or to be made lightly. The more important the ECHR becomes in European law and politics, the greater the need to reflect on the moral foundations of rights and to insist that courts apply consistently principles of interpretation that can be justified as a matter of abstract values of political morality. Such are the demands of pluralism, tolerance, and broadmindedness, without which there is no democratic society.

1

Human Rights, Legality,
and the ECHR

Introduction

What do we need a theory of interpretation of human rights for? Bernard
Williams, who thought that the most important problem of human rights is
that of enforcement not identification, warned that in their efforts to make
the unclear clearer, philosophers often end up making the clear unclear.
'They may', he wrote, 'cause plain truths to disappear into difficult cases,
sensible concepts to dissolve into complex definitions'.[1] While this book
takes Williams's warning seriously, it is motivated by the belief that human
rights theory is essential and it is therefore appropriate that I should begin by
explaining why.

  In this chapter, I set the stage for a theory of interpretation of the ECHR
by locating the Convention within broader issues in human rights theory.
I argue that human rights can play different normative roles in different institutional settings and that failure to distinguish these roles can lead to moral
confusion and political mistakes. Human rights theory is needed not only
because people disagree about whether something is morally right (eg to have
an abortion) but also because they disagree about whether something morally good (eg the eradication of unemployment) is a human right. In this and
the following chapter I argue that out of the many possible normative roles
that human rights can play, the ECHR enshrines human rights that are legal
and liberal: they entail liberal egalitarian principles that impose conditions on
the legitimate use of coercion by Member States. Consequently the European
Court of Human Rights does not exercise illegitimate judicial discretion in
looking for and applying these liberal principles. Later chapters turn to a critical discussion of the methods of interpretation used by the Court in the light
of the values of legality and liberalism.

---

[1] Williams B, *In the Beginning was the Deed* (2005) 64.

Background to and a Very Brief History of Human Rights

The most basic truth about human rights according to Williams lies in what we take to be the most clear and uncontroversial cases of human rights violations, such as torture, executions, and surveillance of the population. Yet these rights are a tiny portion of the rights recognized in international treaties and declarations as human. Here is a non-exhaustive list of the issues labelled as human rights by the United Nations:[2] development, democracy, environment, education, food, globalization (business and human rights), health, housing, water, bioethics (human genome), protection of minorities, protection of indigenous people, protection of persons with disabilities, protection of children, and international solidarity of peoples. It seems paradoxical that the more disputed cases of human rights should far outnumber the clear ones and some philosophical explanation is needed.

It is of course no surprise that the moral foundations of human rights as well as their links with other evaluative concepts of moral and political philosophy—like liberty, equality, or justice—are controversial. The concept of human rights is a relatively recent one which was coined in the late 19th century and entered wider usage only after the Second World War through its role in international law and practice. It is far younger than its elder sibling, the concept of natural rights, which in turn, at least in western thought, post-dates those of justice or democracy. We still continue to make progress—if not politically, then at least philosophically—in our understanding of these older concepts and it would be strange if we had reached consensus on the philosophical underpinnings of such a latecomer in history.

It is useful to look briefly at the history of human rights.[3] Their late arrival in history was no accident. Ideas of human rights emerged in the course of radical changes in the way powerful states practised and viewed international politics as well as in the role of international norms and institutions. These changes were by and large the product of lessons learned by the two world wars of the 20th century and the failure of the pre-1945 regime of international law and politics to prevent them. After the Second World War, powerful states, particularly the victorious allied powers, came to believe that international peace and security depends on domestic protection of individual rights and that a certain degree of international monitoring of domestic practices is not only legitimate but also essential for this purpose. The upshot of these changes

---

[2] See the list on website of the United Nations High Commissioner for Human Rights, at: <http://www.ohchr.org/english/issues/>.

[3] See Freeman M, *Human Rights* (Polity Press, 2002), chs 2 and 3. On the history of the concept of natural rights see Waldron J (ed) *Nonsense on Stilts: Bentham, Burke and Marx on the Rights of Man* (1987).

was the development of the idea that how states treat individuals within their jurisdiction is of legitimate concern to other states and to such a thing as the 'international community'. International human rights embodied this idea through the slogan that individuals have rights 'by virtue of being human'.

To be sure, reference to people's humanity as the basis of rights was not so much (or not only) a natural law rejection of the positivist view held by Bentham, that the only rights which exist are those recognized and enforceable by positive law. Rather, it was meant to convey the idea that a state's international obligations are engaged when it mistreats not only nationals of another state (the international law of aliens) but also its own nationals or stateless groups. This idea signified a departure from the pre-1945 regime of minority protection established by the League of Nations, whose aim was to minimize conflicts between European states triggered by ill-treatment of ethnic minorities living in one state but attached to another.[4] That regime, which was based on inter-state agreements not to mistreat minorities without recognizing individuals as right holders,[5] had failed to prevent war. To assert, in the aftermath of the Second World War, that individuals have rights 'by virtue of being human' was simply to assert that states have obligations by virtue of being members of the international community, with respect to how they treat individuals within their jurisdiction. It was to assert that the notion of state sovereignty was not, if it ever had been, absolute. The exact scope of these obligations as well as the appropriate means of enforcing them were left, and to some extent still remain, unclear.

Critics often like to point out that initially, the international community's preoccupation with how states treat individuals was not motivated by any rational discovery of liberal ideals of individual dignity.[6] Rather, it was triggered by a political assessment that fascist, nationalist, or other totalitarian states are more likely to commit atrocities that pose a threat to international peace and security. This point is to a certain degree true, although contrary to what realist interpretations of international relations might suggest, it says nothing about the contemporary importance of human rights as a value of international law. It is true of course that in 1945, both the USA and the USSR, the two major victorious powers, faced serious human rights violations

[4] On the minority protection regime of the League of Nations see Sohn L and Buergenthal T, *International Protection of Human Rights* (1973) 213.

[5] There was at the time an interesting question as to whether the obligation not to mistreat minorities consisted in treating minorities *equally*, ie in the formal sense of non-discrimination or whether it consisted in treating them *as equals*, ie ensuring the enjoyment of some basic rights for both minorities and the majority alike. The issue came up in the advisory opinion of the Permanent Court of International Justice in *Minority Schools in Albania*, Advisory Opinion No 26, PCIJ, Ser A/B No 64, 1935, which rejected the formal notion of equality as non-discrimination.

[6] See Rorty R, 'Human Rights, Rationality, and Sentimentality' in Shute S, Hurley S (eds) *On Human Rights: the Oxford Amnesty Lectures 1993* (1993) 111.

at home, the former in relation to race discrimination and the latter in relation to large-scale torture, disappearances, and other serious violations of civil rights. It is also true that the rights enshrined in the Universal Declaration of Human Rights and, later on, in the two UN Covenants were the result of political bargaining between primarily western states, a compromised mixture of 17th-century Anglo-American liberal ideals, European socialist ideals, and 20th-century cold war politics.

Still, the somewhat vague consensus on the importance of human rights as a matter of international concern in 1945,[7] instrumental as it may have been, bestowed on the concept a kind of universal moral force that no other concept enjoyed at the international level, certainly not those of democracy or social justice. Democracy in particular (which is nowhere mentioned in the United Nations Charter) could not have been put forward as a value of an organization which was founded on the principle of equality between politically diverse states.[8] It is characteristic that even during the cold war, the radical differences between capitalist and communist states were often represented in terms of a difference of emphasis *within* human rights (the latter privileging social and economic rights at the expense of civil rights) as opposed to a difference between countries that sacrifice human rights and democracy in the name of social justice and those that do not. Given that violation of human rights was the only acceptable ground on which one could get the international community to listen and act legitimately or put pressure on states to promote democracy and economic development, the concept of human rights naturally grew to encompass moral claims that for most states would not traditionally be conceived of as matter of rights.

One could say that, contrary to what happened in the history of western thought and for purely historical reasons, on the international plane, the moral currency of the concept of human rights predated and overshadowed that of justice and democracy. This has led, particularly after the end of the cold war and the gradual process of democratic transition in many Eastern and African states, to an unprecedented proliferation at an international level of what are claimed to be human rights. Whereas in 1945 protection of human rights was seen as a means to promote peace between politically diverse states, after the collapse of the Soviet Union, there was greater recognition of the fact that democratic states do not go to war with each other,[9] do not violate human rights, and do not

---

[7] See the references to human rights in the preamble and in arts 1, 13, 55, 62, and 68 of the United Nations Charter.

[8] See Fox GH and Roth BR, 'Democracy and International Law' 27 *Review of International Studies* (2001) 327–52.

[9] There is a vast literature on the so-called 'democratic peace theory' but see the seminal article by Doyle M, 'Kant, Liberal Legacies and Foreign Affairs' 12 *Philosophy and Public Affairs* (1983) 205.

starve their people. Democracy started to emerge as a value of international law in the early 1990s, essential for securing peace, human rights, and development.[10] But by then, the need to promote these interrelated values had already been expressed in the vocabulary of human rights at the international level due to their long-standing accepted moral currency. This explains both the proliferation of international human rights compared with fewer constitutional rights and the fact that what are called second and third generation human rights are not given protection as legal rights in most western liberal democracies, although they are recognized as acceptable political goals.

We should not therefore lose sight of the fact that there is an important *international* dimension to the concept of human rights. Although human rights are commonly claimed against national governments or against the world as a whole (without identifying the duty holder), they were initially conceived as conditions of legitimacy of states vis-à-vis other states and the international community. They were presented, in other words, as an answer to a specific normative question about which principles should govern international law and practice in a world in which not all states are liberal and democratic. As global politics changed and the aims of the United Nations were revised, human rights assumed different and more diverse normative roles, creating the impression that they constitute a complete moral code for the running of societies and the well-being of people.

No One-Size-Fits-All Theory of Human Rights

Having this international dimension in mind, I think we should draw three distinctions between the way the concept of human rights is used. The first one is between *international* and *national* human rights. It is wrong to assume that the constitutional rights that individuals have by virtue of being citizens of a country must be the same as the rights they have as a matter of international law. Many national constitutions explicitly grant rights that go beyond those owed by all states as a matter of the moral principles governing international relations. Article 16 of the Greek Constitution, for instance, grants a right to free education which at university level shall be provided exclusively by public institutions. Moreover, it is common for the same right to be interpreted differently, often more broadly, by national constitutional courts compared to international human rights bodies.

There is a tendency to equate national and international human rights, both because they overlap to a considerable degree and because in some countries,

---

[10] See Franck T, 'The Emerging Right to Democratic Governance' 86 *American Journal of International Law* (1992).

such as the United Kingdom, international human rights documents have been given a constitutional role as a matter of domestic law. But we should guard against this equation because the question of what a state is committed to as a matter of its constitutional practice and what it owes individuals as a matter of international law are two separate normative questions. There is nothing peculiar about this claim and we are quite familiar with such distinctions in other contexts. As a father, I have a legal duty to provide my kids with the necessary means of subsistence and to look after their well-being. But I do not have a legal duty to love them. This is a moral duty of a different kind. The question of whether the state is justified in punishing me for neglecting my children and the question of whether I have failed as a father are two separate normative questions. The fact that my kids have as much right to my time and money as they have to my love should not obscure this.

Within international human rights there is a further distinction between different normative roles that these rights may play. It is a distinction between accounts of human rights that address their role in setting conditions of international *legitimacy* of states, in the sense of conditions for legitimate toleration by other states, and those that express other legitimate goals that the international community may promote. Consider torture: a state that systematically or routinely tortures people cannot sustain its claim to legitimacy; it cannot tell other states that it is none of their business. Other states are morally justified to interfere through diplomatic pressure, sanctions, or countermeasures, and in extreme circumstances (such as the existence of an ongoing genocide), through military intervention. Now consider democracy and development. Arguably, non-democratic or underdeveloped states that respect civil rights have not lost their claim to legitimate toleration by other states: they are morally justified in opposing and blocking any external interference. Yet both democracy and development are acceptable aims of the international community which are commonly expressed in terms of human rights.

The idea of human rights as setting conditions of justified interference figures prominently in John Rawls's *Law of Peoples*.[11] Rawls explores the important conceptual link between human rights and the propriety of foreign intervention. He proposes a very short list of basic human rights[12] arguing that their protection meets the conditions for international toleration. At first glance, Rawls's proposal seems to contradict the widely held view within the United Nations human rights system, that there is no formal hierarchy of human rights

---

[11] Rawls J *The Law of Peoples* (1999) 80. See the discussion in the next section.

[12] These are: '[R]ight to life (to the means of subsistence and security); to liberty (to freedom from slavery, serfdom and forced occupation, and to a sufficient measure of liberty of conscience to ensure freedom of religion and thought); to property (personal property); and to formal equality as expressed by rules of natural justice (that is, that similar cases be treated similarly).' *Law of Peoples*, at 65.

and that all human rights, of all generations, are indivisible, interdependent, and interrelated.[13] Yet there is no contradiction as the idea of indivisibility of human rights addresses a different normative question to that of legitimate toleration, namely, whether all human rights promote moral values that are equally important for the well-being of individuals. Not all rights that are called human rights perform the same normative role. In fact, even the scope of the same right may vary depending on which normative role it performs. Consider freedom of expression: absolute censorship of political opposition by a state is a legitimate ground of interference by other states and the international community, but laws prohibiting the denial of the holocaust are not.[14] It is therefore wrong to speak of a hierarchy of human rights as if this is a hierarchy within the same normative role. We do better to speak of different, equally important, normative roles that rights of international law play and we are quite familiar with this idea from the concepts of *erga omnes* and *jus cogens* in international law.[15] Rawls's idea that states must meet some minimal standards to be accepted to the society of Peoples finds considerable support in the concept of obligations *erga omnes*[16] which includes only some human rights obligations.

There is yet another distinction that cuts across the first two, between human rights as *legal* rights and human rights as *political* goals. If I have a legal right, it means that I am morally entitled to be treated in the way this right requires. It means that the state has a duty not to use coercion in a way that would violate this right and that the benefits of the principles that underlie this right should be extended to all.[17] If I am denied this right, I am harmed

---

[13] See paragraph 5 of the UN Vienna Declaration and Programme of Action adopted at the Second World Conference on Human Rights in 1993: 'All human rights are universal, indivisible and interdependent and interrelated. The international community must treat human rights globally in a fair and equal manner, on the same footing, and with the same emphasis. While the significance of national and regional particularities and various historical, cultural and religious backgrounds must be borne in mind, it is the duty of States, regardless of their political, economic and cultural systems, to promote and protect all human rights and fundamental freedoms.'

[14] Dworkin's example, in *Is Democracy Possible Here?* (2006) 34.

[15] On the issue of the hierarchy of international human rights and its relation to *erga omnes* and *jus cogens* norms see: Meron T, 'On a Hierarchy of International Human Rights' 80 *American Journal of International Law* (1986) 1; Koji T, 'Emerging Hierarchy in International Human Rights and Beyond: From the Perspective of Non-Derogable Rights' 12 *European Journal of International Law* (2001) 917.

[16] Cf the definition of *erga omnes* obligations in the International Criminal Tribunal for the Former Yugoslavia (ICTY) case of *Prosecutor v Anto Furundzija* (1998), Case No IT-95–17/1-T, para 151: 'The prohibition of torture imposes upon States obligations *erga omnes*, that is, obligations owed towards all the other members of the international community, each of which then has a correlative right. In addition, the violation of such an obligation simultaneously constitutes a breach of the correlative right of all members of the international community and gives rise to a claim for compliance accruing to each and every member, which then has the right to insist on fulfilment of the obligation or in any case to call for the breach to be discontinued'.

[17] Dworkin R, *Justice in Robes* (2006) 13.

in a special way, over and above the harm done to me by not receiving the treatment. Suppose that the right to vote and to stand for elections is a legal right that is enshrined in the constitution. Suppose further that the principle justifying this right is (roughly) the democratic principle that we should all have the opportunity to have a say on how we are governed and to influence which policies are adopted, regardless of the political views each one of us holds. If the government denies me the right to vote or stand for elections on the grounds that my views are unpopular, then it offends the very principle that justifies why *anybody* should have the right to vote. The moral harm is double. First, I was deprived of the opportunity to influence the outcome of the elections, in violation of democratic principles. Secondly, coercion was used in an unprincipled way: no principle could be found to justify why my vote was not taken into account but that of other people was.

Now contrast this to a situation where my vote had no impact in the election outcome due to a good-faith counting mistake that could have been prevented if more resources had been spent or officials had received more training. My complaint here is different. It cannot be that the government used coercion in an unprincipled way, for the occurrence of the counting mistake did not offend the principle underlying the right to vote. It may of course offend some other moral principle stemming from the value of democracy, but unless that principle underlies other legal rights coercively enforced, then my only complaint is that more could be done to enhance democracy by improving the counting process.

The language of human rights is often used to state political (moral) goals that are not legal rights. Presumably, a state should try to avoid counting errors in the electoral process by providing training and spending resources. Avoiding such errors would be a good thing. It would enhance and promote democracy. But it does not follow that my legal right to vote includes a right that my vote is not miscounted, that—should this happen—the government harms me by using coercion in an unprincipled manner and I should receive compensation. A legal right to something does not entail an entitlement to the maximization of the value that right serves. Politically of course, we understand the claim that there is a human right to democracy and we can agree that states must take measures to ensure that the counting process in an election is to a reasonable extent free from errors. To put it crudely: there is more to human rights than human rights law.[18]

We should note how failure to draw these distinctions can cause great moral confusion and political mistakes. People who live in undemocratic regimes

---

[18] On the issue of the so-called legalization of human rights see Meckled-Garcia S and Cali B (eds) *The Legalisation of Human Rights* (2005).

that meet the conditions of legitimate tolerance may be outraged by the lack of external intervention and feel that the international community does not care about their human rights. People who do not enjoy some international human rights (eg social and economic) as a matter of constitutional law in their country may feel that their state is violating their human rights. People whose 'human rights' interests could have been better served by a different legislative policy may feel that their legal rights have been violated and feel entitled to compensation. These unfounded complaints that sadly are becoming more and more frequent, are motivated by the belief that whenever there is a human right to something, its moral force and the duties it assigns are fixed. But this is a mistake. *There is no 'one-size-fits-all' theory of human rights, either of their moral foundations or of their scope.* Human rights perform different roles in different institutional contexts. It might of course have been preferable to restrict the use of the concept 'human rights' to the promotion of one value or the performance of one role in political morality (perhaps the most pressing one) but, for the reasons explained earlier, this battle has been long lost if it was ever properly fought.

We might as well say that there are different *concepts* of human rights and that someone claiming a human right had better explain what he or she means. Suppose I believe that Turkey's banning of headscarves in public spaces[19] is not a violation of human rights because it does not breach Turkey's entitlement to legitimate toleration and does not justify any kind of intervention by international organizations or other states. You agree but you also believe, as I do, that the ban on headscarves violates liberal democratic principles that Turkey should aspire to. If I claim that women have no human right to wear a headscarf in Turkey and you say that they do, then we are talking past each other. We seem to be disagreeing but we actually aren't. Both of us think that the ban on headscarves violates liberal democratic principles, and both of us think that this violation does not justify any kind of intervention. But now suppose that you think that the ban on headscarves does call for some kind of intervention by the international community and I think it does not. Here we do disagree, but not on whether the right to wear one's religious symbols is a good thing. We disagree on the role of the international community (or particular international organizations) and the normative limits of their intervention; if you insist on there being a right to wear one's religious symbols from a liberal point of view, then you have simply begged that very important question.

It seems to me that many people are sceptical about certain human rights (for instance, minority rights or social and economic rights), not because they

---

[19] See the European Court of Human Rights case of *Leyla Sahin v Turkey*, Application No 44774/98, Judgment of 10 November 2005.

reject the goals that these rights promote but because they disagree with what they think would follow were these goals to be recognized as human rights. Many human rights activists for instance complain about the inadequate *judicial* protection of social and economic rights. One does not have to be a libertarian to oppose the judicial protection of social and economic rights. It is an open question whether judicial protection of these rights better serves the value that underlies them. We can of course understand human rights campaigners who think that there should be more free speech in undemocratic states; who think that social and economic rights should be incorporated into national constitutions and that states should do more to improve the welfare of their people; and who think that courts should assume a role in promoting human rights goals. But unless they specify the nature of the moral complaint and who should do what about it, then their human rights claims are vague, unhelpful and, often, populist expressions of political views disguised as matters of principle.

In the light of these three distinctions above and the moral confusion that the different senses of human rights can create, it seems to me that it is important, both philosophically and normatively, to locate the ECHR rights under the appropriate category with a view to identify the principles that should govern its interpretation and application.

Human Rights as Conditions of Legitimacy

When John Rawls published the *Law of Peoples* many were surprised by the stark differences between his theory of international justice and his earlier theory of domestic justice. Whereas he had defended a principle of egalitarian redistribution in the domestic case (what he called the difference principle), Rawls rejected such a principle for international justice, advocating instead a duty of well-ordered[20] peoples to assist societies burdened by unfavourable conditions, in their effort to become well-ordered too. Moreover, although he defended the principle that all peoples must honour human rights, he provided a rather short list of human rights, insisting that they are not the same as constitutional rights or rights of liberal democratic citizenship. Human rights in the *Law of Peoples*, Rawls argued, are a special class of *urgent* rights whose role is to restrict the justifying reasons for war and to specify limits to a regime's internal autonomy. They are rights not politically parochial which can and should be honoured by non-liberal peoples. 'An agreement on a Law of Peoples ensuring human rights', Rawls writes, 'is not an agreement limited

---

[20] There are two kinds of well-ordered peoples: liberal peoples and decent hierarchical societies. See Rawls J, *Law of Peoples*, at 4.

only to liberal societies'. Rawls assigns the following three roles to human rights in the Law of Peoples:[21]

1. Their fulfilment is a necessary condition of the decency of a society's political institutions and of its legal order.
2. Their fulfilment is sufficient to exclude justified and forceful intervention by other peoples, for example, by diplomatic and economic sanctions, or in grave cases by military force.
3. They set a limit to the pluralism among peoples.

The account of human rights that flows from these normative roles is significantly narrower in scope compared to that of constitutional rights of a liberal state or to the inflated scope of all the human rights found in international treaties and declarations. For example, the denial of full and equal liberty of conscience or religion (for instance, prohibiting adherents to certain religions from holding certain positions or using certain forms of expression, both of which are allowed to adherents to the dominant religion) need not be a violation of Rawlsian human rights while it is undeniably a violation of liberal constitutional rights. As to the rights found in international treaties and declarations, particularly second and third generation rights, these are certainly far more extensive than Rawls's basic right to subsistence.[22] In sum, Rawls offers an account of human rights which is *minimalist* both in its justification[23] and its scope: human rights must be such that they can be accepted by non-liberal peoples and are fewer than the rights of a liberal democratic state.

Rawls is not alone in going minimalist about human rights. Williams too thought that human rights should not be given a liberal foundation. He wrote: 'It seems to me sensible, both philosophically and politically, to make our views about human rights, or at least the most basic human rights, depend as little as possible on disputable theses of liberalism or any other particular ideology'.[24] Dworkin too distinguishes between human rights and liberal rights (which he calls political) on the grounds that the former protect individuals only against acts of government that cannot be thought to be justified by any intelligible conception of human dignity.[25]

---

[21] ibid at 80.

[22] Of course some international human rights may be conducive to meeting the conditions Rawls specifies for well-ordered societies (eg that individuals' basic needs are met) or be interpreted as what well-ordered peoples owe to burdened societies, but it seems to me that overall they are much more ambitious than that.

[23] On justificatory minimalism see Cohen J, 'Minimalism About Human Rights: the Best We Can Hope For?' 12 *Journal of Political Philosophy* (2004) 190.

[24] Williams B, *In the Beginning was the Deed* (2005) at 74.

[25] Dworkin R, *Is Democracy Possible Here?* 'We do better to explain the idea of human rights, I suggest, not by trying to establish grades of damage that governments inflict when they make good-faith mistakes in identifying people's moral rights but instead by distinguishing good-faith

Are these philosophers right to distinguish human rights from liberal constitutional rights in this way? And if so, does it follow that the scope of the ECHR should be construed narrowly? I believe that these are two separate questions and that our answer to the second question does not depend on our answer to the first. In fact, Rawls's account of human rights is not incompatible with the United Nations promoting the more liberal rights of western liberal democracies. Let me explain.

Rawls's moral methodology is premised on the idea that 'the correct regulative principle for a thing depends on the nature of that thing'[26] and that morality is multilayered.[27] As a result, different principles govern practices whose circumstances and features differ from a moral point of view. It need not be the case, for example, that the principles governing relations between peoples include a principle of egalitarian redistribution to the worst-off, just because the latter governs relations between free and equal citizens.

Now, the roles that Rawls assigns to human rights address the question of the appropriate foreign policy of liberal peoples and the international community towards non-liberal peoples. It does not address the question whether liberal principles are normatively superior to the principles of decent hierarchical peoples nor whether liberal rights are normatively superior to human rights. It is therefore wrong to suggest, as some philosophers have,[28] that Rawls's minimalist account of human rights necessarily competes with more loaded theories of human rights that promote liberal egalitarian ideals. We need not deny that within liberal democratic states, human rights do have this morally loaded character, nor that the international community may promote liberal human rights by helping states that show commitment to them. What I called human rights as political goals, which go beyond Rawls's minimalist account of human rights, may have precisely that function without contradicting the *Law of Peoples*. In fact, part of what the United Nations does about human rights (for instance, sanctions authorized by the Security Council or the establishment of ad hoc international tribunals) may perform

---

mistakes made by governments that respect human dignity in principle from those acts that show only contempt for or indifference to human dignity', at 33–5.

[26] Rawls J, *A Theory of Justice*, revised edn (Harvard University Press 1999) 25.

[27] For a discussion and a defence of Rawls's approach, see Nagel T, 'The Problem of Global Justice' 33 (No 2) *Philosophy and Public Affairs* (2005) 113.

[28] For the criticism that Rawls's account of human rights is unjustifiably restricted, see Buchanan A, 'Rawls's Law of Peoples: Rules for a Vanished Westphalian World' 110 *Ethics* (July 2000) 697; Beitz CR, 'Rawls's Law of Peoples', 110 *Ethics* (July 2000) 669, at 683–8; Nickel J, 'Human Rights', *Stanford Encyclopedia of Philosophy*, available at <http://plato.stanford.edu/entries/rights-human/>. I am not sure however whether there is actually a disagreement here. At times, both Beitz and Nickel seem to object that the conventional use of the concept of human rights is broader than Rawls's. But these other uses of the concept of human rights need not refer to the same normative question and can therefore be compatible with the *Law of Peoples*.

Rawls's role of legitimate toleration and another part of the United Nations (eg the General Comments of the Human Rights Committee and the various UN General Assembly declarations) the role of setting liberal political goals for states already committed to liberal principles. Rawls, as I understand him, gives a theory of legitimate tolerance of peoples in a world in which not all peoples are liberal; he does not give a theory of what human rights people have in a liberal democracy, or a theory of why non-liberal states do not grant their people all the rights that they ideally should as a matter of political morality.

It is therefore an open question whether the ECHR rights should be seen as merely setting conditions for legitimate toleration of states in Europe, whether they should be seen as enshrining rights of a liberal democratic state, or as doing *both* depending on the state in question.[29] We can say, in the same breath, that minimalism about human rights suits most of the United Nations charter-based model, whereas liberalism about human rights suits most of Europe's law-based model. Many features of the ECHR, beginning with its wording[30] and the fact that it is a *regional* convention whose Member States are now all committed—at least in theory—to liberal democracy,[31] suggest that its role goes beyond that of setting conditions of legitimate toleration. But in fact a stronger argument in this direction stems from the long-standing role of the ECHR rights as legal rights against the government of Contracting States, to which I now turn.

Human Rights, Legal Rights, and Interpretivism

What does one have by virtue of having a legal right? Does the answer differ in the case of international human rights? Ronald Dworkin has argued that what the law of a particular jurisdiction requires or prohibits or permits is a normative question: the answer depends on the best interpretation of a shared practice which we take to have value even though we do not agree on what this value is and what it entails. He calls concepts that refer to shared practices which have these features 'interpretive' and he argues that the central concepts

---

[29] This third option should remain open as a possibility and in fact it may be used to defend the idea of the 'margin of appreciation' which many people confuse with a doctrine of cultural relativism. There is nothing wrong in principle about this third option, although, as I will argue, it is incompatible with the status of the ECHR as a source of legal rights and duties. See ch 6.

[30] The preamble of the ECHR reads that the signatories reaffirm 'their profound belief in those fundamental freedoms which are the foundation of justice and peace in the world and are best maintained on the one hand by an effective political democracy and on the other by a common understanding and observance of the human rights upon which they defend'.

[31] For a discussion of the relationship between the ECHR and democracy see Marks S, 'The European Convention on Human Rights and its "democratic society"' 66 *British Yearbook of International Law* (1995) 209.

of political morality such as justice, democracy, liberty, and equality, are also interpretive. Unlike criterial concepts (like the concept of bachelorhood) and natural kind concepts (like the concept of water) the correct application of interpretive concepts is not determined by convergent linguistic practice but by the best interpretation of the value of the practice in which they figure. Such interpretation is bound to be controversial and insensitive to how most people talk and what they think.

The value of political morality that the concept of law refers to (which Dworkin calls *legality* or the *rule of law)* has state coercion as its focus. It refers to the conditions under which the use of coercive force by the state is legitimate. 'Law', Dworkin writes, 'insists that force not be used or withheld, no matter how useful that would be to ends in view, no matter how beneficial or noble those ends, except as licensed or required by individual rights and responsibilities flowing from past political decisions about when collective force is justified'.[32] The value of legality governs when the use of collective force is legitimate.[33] The best understanding of the value of legality lies for Dworkin in the ideal of political *integrity*: states should govern through a coherent set of political principles whose benefit extends to all citizens.

I take Dworkin's account of law in the domestic case to be largely correct[34] both in arguing that legal practice is governed by a distinctive value of political morality and that law as integrity is the best conception of this value. I will not defend it in great detail in this book except in the sense that I believe it is instantiated in the practice of the ECHR.[35] The question I am interested in is whether and how it can be extended to international legal practice and the case of the ECHR in particular. This depends on the extent to which that practice shares the same morally relevant features with the national one and whether any additional features that it has make a moral difference. There are two crucial stages. The first stage is to examine whether the practice of the ECHR is an interpretive one. Do we share a practice whereby we converge in treating the concept of the ECHR law as interpretive? Does the practice

---

[32] Dworkin R, *Law's Empire* (1986), at 93.

[33] For critical discussion of the connection between law and state coercion in the context of Dworkin's attack on legal positivism, see Dickson J, 'Methodology in Jurisprudence: A Critical Survey' 10 *Legal Theory* (2004) 117, at 141ff.

[34] For critical discussion of Dworkin's work see the collected essays in Hershovitz S (ed) *Exploring Law's Empire: The Jurisprudence of Ronald Dworkin* (2006) and in Burley J (ed) *Dworkin and His Critics* (2004), chs 14–17.

[35] This is of course no argument in favour of Dworkin's theory, as whether or not law as integrity is the best theory of law is ultimately a question of political morality. It is not a question of extracting theories from the bare facts of practices, such that the more practices we find like the ones Dworkin describes the more likely it is that his theory is correct. I am indebted to discussions with Nicos Stavropoulos on this and to his 'Why Principles' (unpublished manuscript on file with author).

invite us to reflect on what rights the ECHR creates without being committed to the notion that all or virtually all lawyers use the same criteria for identifying these rights? Or is it the case that the concept of the ECHR law is exhausted by the tests lawyers share for deciding what the ECHR requires? No doubt, whether or not a theory of interpretation of the ECHR is a viable project depends on the practice of the ECHR being interpretive in this sense. The second stage is to look at the possible values that can be attributed to the ECHR rights, assuming that the concept is interpretive. This task is one of examining which account of human rights best fits and justifies the practice of the ECHR, seen in the light of the value of legality.

It may be objected that Dworkin's theory of law was meant to apply to municipal law and cannot be extended to the interpretation of international law and the ECHR in particular.[36] There are indeed some complications here: it appears that unlike national law, international law does not regulate how state coercion will be used against individuals but how states treat each other in the absence of a world legislature, executive, and judiciary. Being an international treaty—the objection goes—the ECHR lacks the attributes of legality, as we know it in municipal law. There is, first, no obligation under the ECHR to incorporate the convention into domestic law such that national courts condition the deploying of Member States' monopoly of coercive force on what the ECHR requires. The Convention has this effect in monist Member States but need not have such effect in dualist states,[37] like the United Kingdom. Secondly, the European Court of Human Rights does not have any coercive powers similar to powers of judicial review that national constitutional courts have. It cannot disapply or strike down legislation or order executive action. Its judgments are not directly enforceable at domestic level. On an extremely realist view of international law, the combination of these elements might suggest that the ECHR is not 'really' law: states are sovereign to decide whether to join the ECHR, whether to incorporate it, and whether to comply with the judgments of the European Court of Human Rights. How can the duty not

[36] Lord Hoffmann made this point recently in a case concerning the right to a fair trial under art 6 ECHR and the international law on state immunity: 'As Professor Dworkin demonstrated in *Law's Empire* (1986), the ordering of competing principles according to the importance of the values which they embody is a basic technique of adjudication. But the same approach cannot be adopted in international law, which is based upon the common consent of nations. It is not for a national court to "develop" international law by unilaterally adopting a version of that law which, however desirable, forward-looking and reflective of values it may be, is simply not accepted by other states'; *Jones v Ministry of Interior Al-Mamlaka Al-Arabiya AS Saudiya (the Kingdom of Saudi Arabia) and Others* [2006] UKHL 26, para 63.
[37] There is some considerable difficulty in drawing the distinction between monist and dualist states in relation to the ECHR, which has become more blurred as Luzius Wildhaber, the past president of the European Court of Human Rights, remarks in 'The European Convention on Human Rights and International Law' 56 *International and Comparative Law Quarterly* (2006) 217.

to violate the ECHR be legal when no one can force states to do any of those things? Is it not, at best, a matter of good political will of Member States? A *promise* made to other States to respect the ECHR, as opposed to a legal duty they have towards their own citizens?

Such suggestions would be wrong for several reasons. To begin with, state consent is neither a sufficient nor a necessary condition for the creation of an international legal duty. So called peremptory norms of international law (eg norms prohibiting war, crimes against humanity, slavery, or torture), bind a state regardless of and even against its will. Besides, it would be wholly circular to argue that state consent is the ultimate foundation of international law because states consent that it is. Some value, like the value of equality and autonomy of peoples, must justify the importance of the *fact* of state consent and in doing so, it will necessarily shape and limit its justificatory role. States are indeed free not to join or to withdraw from international human rights treaties like the ECHR, but it does not follow that they are not bound anyway by some of the human rights enshrined therein.

It is a mistake moreover to equate law with the existence of sanctions. As HLA Hart's attack on Austin's command theory of law teaches us, the existence of a legal norm is the reason for the imposition of sanctions rather than the other way around.[38] Legal obligation cannot be reduced to directing officials to impose sanctions, as the law (eg criminal and tort law) tells us not to act in a certain way in the first place, as opposed to what will happen if we do. Moreover, not all legal consequences are sanctions for breach of duty (eg the annulment of a voidable contract) and not all legal duties are coupled by sanctions (eg the duty of higher courts to apply the law). The same holds in the case of the ECHR: the Convention does not tell states that they will be ordered to pay compensation if they violate the ECHR. It tells states not to violate the ECHR in the first place. Recall art 1 of the ECHR: 'The High Contracting Parties shall secure to everyone within their jurisdiction the rights and freedoms defined in Section I of this Convention'.[39] We can say, quite plausibly, that the question of which rights and duties the Convention creates is independent of which courts have jurisdiction to interpret and apply it. As in domestic law, a theory of law is prior to, and not coextensive with, a theory of adjudication.[40]

[38] Hart HLA, *The Concept of Law,* 2nd edn (1994), pp 27–42.

[39] Cf the corresponding provision in art 2 of the International Covenant on Civil and Political Rights (ICCPR): 'Each State Party to the present Covenant undertakes to respect and to ensure to all individuals within its territory and subject to its jurisdiction the rights recognized in the present Covenant, without distinction of any kind, such as race, colour, sex, language, religion, political or other opinion, national or social origin, property, birth or other status'.

[40] This was an early, and quite common, misunderstanding of Dworkin's argument in *Law's Empire.* See the discussion in Dworkin, *Justice in Robes,* pp 18–21.

The principle behind the idea of a primary obligation not to violate the ECHR is exhibited, I believe, in the binding force of interim measures which was recognized recently by the ECtHR.[41] It is also reflected in the concept of 'pilot judgments' that was recently introduced by the European Court following a resolution of the Committee of Ministers.[42] In the landmark *Broniowski v Poland*,[43] the Court did not simply hold that Poland was in breach of Protocol 1 art 1 ECHR. It also held that the violation 'originated in a systemic problem connected with the malfunctioning of domestic legislation and practice' and that 'the respondent State must, through appropriate legal measures and administrative practices, secure the implementation of the property right in question'.[44] Although the device of a 'pilot judgment' is meant to target the problem of repetitive or clone cases that jeopardize the effectiveness of the Strasbourg machinery, it does however suggest that the obligations the ECHR creates *constrain whether and how domestic political decisions (eg domestic statutes or judicial decisions) license state coercion*.[45] It is difficult to argue that the ECHR does not impose any obligations on states in relation to repealing or amending legislation that violates human rights principles.

It is wrong moreover to suggest that the Convention need not have any direct effect in dualist states. Under art 13 of the ECHR, all Member States have a duty to provide effective remedies before a national authority for everyone whose ECHR rights and freedoms are violated. For example, the United Kingdom was found in breach of art 13 ECHR, in relation to the test used in judicial review of administrative action.[46] As the Court notes, the effect of art 13 ECHR is to 'require the provision of a domestic remedy allowing the "competent national authority" both to deal with the substance of the relevant

---

[41] See *Mamatkulov and Askarov v Turkey* (Grand Chamber), Judgment of 4 February 2005, Reports of Judgments and Decisions 2005-I. Member States have a primary duty, under the Convention, not to cause irreparable harm to individuals, as opposed merely to provide a remedy should this occur. The duty is of course qualified, subject to further conditions such as knowledge and likelihood of the harm being irreparable. See the discussion in Letsas G, 'International Human Rights and the Binding Force of Interim Measures' 5 *European Human Rights Law Review* (2003) 527.

[42] Resolution of the Committee of Ministers on judgments revealing an underlying systemic problem, Res (2004) 3, 12 May 2004.

[43] *Broniowski v Poland*, Judgment of 11 June 2004; 40 EHRR 495. See also the later judgments in *Hutten-Czapsak v Poland* (App 35014/97), Judgment of 19 June 2006.

[44] ibid, point 4 of the *dispotif*.

[45] In his separate Opinion in *Broniowski* at point 4 of the *Dispositif*, Judge Zupančič argued that the rationale of using pilot judgments to address systemic violations has nothing to do with the problem of the caseload and 'everything to do with justice'.

[46] This was before the coming into force of the Human Rights Act 1998, in relation to the 'Wednesbury' test of irrationality which did not include a test of proportionality. See *Smith and Grady v United Kingdom*, Judgment of 27 September 1999; (2000) 29 EHRR 493.

Convention complaint and to grant appropriate relief'.[47] Interestingly, the European Court of Human Rights does not interpret the right to an effective remedy under art 13 to entail a duty to allow review of national legislation when the latter is the source of the grievance, as this would amount to an obligation to incorporate the Convention.[48] Be that as it may, the primary duty to respect the Convention rights under art 1 and the duty to provide effective remedies under art 13 show that the ECHR penetrates the national legal order, quite independently of the existence of the European Court of Human Rights and its powers.[49] Recall that under the principle of subsidiarity, the role of international human rights bodies is subsidiary to the institutions of the national legal order.[50] The failure of national authorities to comply with human rights does not mean that the ECHR is not 'really law' any more than the failure of national courts to apply national law, or the failure of the executive to comply with the law or with a judgment of a national court means that national law is not really law.

Some scholars insist that the most important features of the ECHR which distinguish it from other international human rights treaties and earn it its status as law, are to be found in arts 32, 34, and 46 ECHR. These provide that the jurisdiction of the ECtHR to receive individual applications and to interpret and apply the Convention is compulsory for all Member States and that the final judgment of the Court shall be binding on the Respondent State. Anne-Marie Slaughter and Lawrence Helfer, for example, take the ECHR to be an instance of *supranational*, as opposed to *international*, adjudication. Supranational adjudication is characterized by the existence of 'international organizations empowered to exercise some of the functions otherwise reserved to states'.[51] Slaughter and Helfer group the ECHR together with the European Union and argue that, unlike international organizations, these supranational institutions are marked by a greater transfer of or limitation on state sovereignty involved in their establishment, and by the ability to make decisions

---

[47] See *Peck v United Kingdom*, Judgment of 28 January 2003; (2003) 36 EHRR 719, para 99. Note, however, that a 'competent national authority' need not be a judicial one.

[48] See *A and Others v United Kingdom*, Judgment of 17 December 2002; (2003) 36 EHRR 917, para 112: 'the Court reiterates that Article 13 does not go so far as to guarantee a remedy allowing a Contracting State's primary legislation to be challenged before a national authority on grounds that it is contrary to the Convention'.

[49] On the influence of the Convention on Member States see Bernhard R, 'The convention and domestic law' in Macdonald, Matscher, and Petzold (eds) *The European System for the Protection of Human Rights* (1993) 25.

[50] On the principle of subsidiarity in the ECHR see Petzold H, 'The Convention and the Principle of Subsidiarity' in Macdonald, Matscher, and Petzold (eds), *The European System for the Protection of Human Rights* (1993) 41.

[51] See their seminal article, Helfer L and Slaughter AM, 'Towards a Theory of Effective Supranational Adjudication' 107(2) *Yale Law Journal* (1997) 287.

which are directly binding upon Member States as well as individuals within these states.

It seems to me that the distinction between international and supranational levels is sound and that supranational law is governed by the same principles as municipal law. But I do not believe that we should draw this distinction on the basis of the right of individual petition and the binding character of a supranational court's decisions. Adjudication is a red herring. It seems to me that there are two elements which are crucial for the status of the ECHR rights as legal rights that have the same moral status as constitutional rights. The first is the subject matter and the holder of the ECHR rights and duties. As we saw, the ECHR (and the ICCPR for that matter) grants rights that condition the way in which states use coercion against individuals within their jurisdiction. If Member states have a legal obligation not to act in violation of the ECHR (in legislative, executive, and judicial functions) then it follows that no proposition of law is true as a matter of domestic law unless it is compatible with the ECHR. The ECHR is part of the normative materials that make each and every proposition of domestic law true. In this respect, the ECHR rights are exactly like the constitutional rights of Member States.[52] The fact that not all domestic courts can take the ECHR into account in deciding propositions of law makes no difference. In many states (France for instance) lower courts do not have jurisdiction to interpret and apply constitutional rights. It does not follow that the truth conditions of propositions of law (say, whether it is true that I have the legal right to burn my country's flag in public) *change* when the case goes from the lower courts to the higher ones. This aspect of the ECHR is very different from other international law treaties (eg trade agreements) that regulate activities between states without aiming at binding states towards their own citizens in relation to how they use coercion. As the European Commission has noted:

the obligations undertaken by the High Contracting Parties in the Convention are essentially of an objective character, being designed rather to protect the fundamental rights of individual human beings from infringement by any of the High Contracting Parties than to create subjective and reciprocal rights for the High Contracting Parties themselves.[53]

The second element pertinent to the legal standing of the ECHR rights refers to the attitude of the relevant actors: are the ECHR rights treated by states,

---

[52] For the opposite argument, that the ECHR is not part of a broader constitutional arrangement see Mahoney P, 'Judicial Activism and Judicial Self-Restraint in the European Court of Human Rights: two sides of the same coin' 11 *Human Rights Law Journal* (1990) 57.

[53] *Austria v Italy*, App No 788/60, Yearbook of the European Court of Human Rights (1961) Vol 4, 140.

individuals and courts as rights that condition the use of coercive force as a matter of law? As I will argue in Chapter 2, this condition is met in the case of ECHR. One important feature of the ECHR which has encouraged this attitude, and which other international human rights treaties like the ICCPR lack, is that the decisions of the European Court of Human Rights are binding and the record of compliance with its judgment has been very strong. But it is the attitude that matters, not how it came about.[54] Member States treat the judgments of the European Court of Human Rights as a reason to amend or repeal national legislation with a view to comply with their obligation under art 1 of the ECHR.

Conclusion

We live in a period in which human rights claims and theories of human rights abound. In this chapter, I have tried to distinguish between the many different normative roles that the concept of human rights can play and to make space for a distinctive normative framework within which the ECHR can be located. The failure to take up this philosophical task risks moral confusion and political mistakes. Unlike the role of human rights in theories of global justice, the purpose of the ECHR is not to set conditions for the legitimate tolerance of states. And unlike the role of human rights in the work of international human rights bodies, the purpose of the ECHR is not to set acceptable political goals that all states have a reason to promote, albeit at their own discretion. Rather, the point and purpose of the ECHR can be located in the value of legality, ie the value which governs when the use of the state's coercive power against its people is legitimate. By attributing this point to the ECHR, we can equate the normative role of the Convention rights with that of liberal rights within the national constitutional order. While the status of the ECHR as an international treaty raises some challenges against this equation, these challenges can be met and need not stand in the way of constructing a theory of interpretation which applies to the ECHR but not to other parts of international law.

---

[54] It is important to stress this point as it would be wrong to argue that a text becomes a source of law because a court has duty to take it into account, and the judgments of the court are binding on the parties. It is the other way around.

2

Autonomous Concepts, Conventionalism, and Judicial Discretion

Introduction

We want our courts to get the law right. For most of us, the courts have a duty to apply the law and nothing but the law. We do not want innocent people to go to prison or lose their money. We take great care to ensure that the facts of each case will be fully assessed and the law will be properly applied to them. In most of the cases that courts decide, this is of utmost importance mainly to the litigant parties. Most of us are lucky enough to spend our lives without ever having to face a lawsuit or stand accused of a crime and we may not be particularly concerned with how justice is administered. We are of course very much concerned with what laws are passed—our well-being depends on them—but we hope that we will enjoy our legal rights and perform our legal duties outside courtrooms.

Sometimes we stand to gain or lose not because the government has passed a law granting a new right or imposed a new duty but because higher courts have ruled on a controversial question of law. Millions of people may be affected by what a higher court decides on a hard case of tax law. It is therefore important in such cases, and not just for the litigants, that judges reason well. But outside constitutional law, it is not the end of the world if they do not, because in a liberal democracy, citizens adversely affected can put pressure on the government to enact clear legislation and overrule the courts. They are more likely to do that than accuse judges of incompetence or judicial activism.

Things are very different however when courts have the final authority to interpret and apply the constitution, including the fundamental rights enshrined therein. Most of us care a great deal about what constitutional rights we have against the government, and about what the government may or may not do. We care not only when we are personally affected but as a matter of principle. But while we may feel strongly about the rights we think we have, we do realize that in many cases people who disagree with us hold their views

with as much honesty, passion, and good faith as we do. When constitutional courts have the final authority to strike down or disapply legislation that, in their view, violates these constitutional rights, then their role will inevitably become the subject of political controversies. The more significant a role a court has, the more likely it is that concerns will be raised about the limits of its powers and the politics that lie behind its judgments.

Does the role of international human rights bodies approximate that of constitutional courts in this respect? It is difficult to see how. Many such bodies, like the former UN Commission on Human Rights (which was replaced by the Human Rights Council) do not have judicial functions and do not hear individual applications. Their primary function is to examine information relevant to gross violations of human rights and to put diplomatic pressure on states to end them. As in the case of international criminal courts (like the International Criminal Court), their role is not so much to decide what rights we have in the face of controversy, but to establish facts regarding gross violations of basic and uncontroversial rights. In other words, they mainly deal with questions of fact, not questions of law, and with issues of human rights enforcement, not human rights interpretation. But even in the case of quasi-judicial bodies 'like the UN Human Rights Committee', decisions reached on individual petitions are not binding on states and are quite frequently ignored by the respondent state. Although some of its decisions (called 'views') involve controversial issues of human rights interpretation, most focus on applying the text of the International Covenant on Civil and Political Rights (ICCPR) to specific factual situations.[1] They are relatively short and receive very little publicity.

The European Court of Human Rights (ECtHR) however is an exception. Although there was no right of direct access to the Court until the reform of the 11th Protocol in 1998, its judgments have always enjoyed publicity and respect amongst contracting states. There are several reasons behind this success, summarized succinctly by Anne-Marie Slaughter and Laurence Helfer.[2] Some of these reasons are sociological: they refer to social facts about the European Court (composition, capacities, quality of its reasoning, and binding force of its judgments) and about the Contracting States (nature of violations that they face, cultural homogeneity in Europe). These reasons help to explain, in a descriptive and socio-scientific sense, why the European human rights system has been so effective.

But there are other facts which are important from a *normative* rather than a descriptive point of view. This means that when these facts occur they alter

---

[1] Helfer L, Slaughter AM, 'Towards a Theory of Effective Supranational Adjudication' 107(2) *Yale Law Journal* (1997) 382.

[2] ibid at 298–337.

our moral landscape—for instance what rights and duties we have and what the relevant actors should do. In the case of the ECHR, such facts explain not only why the European Court has been very effective in protecting human rights but also why it is *justified* in doing so. What are these facts? First, that the Convention is widely treated (by states, individuals, and courts) as a source of important rights and duties which courts must get right as a matter of *law*. Secondly, that the status of the ECHR rights as justiciable rights against the government is treated as morally significant when it comes to interpreting their scope and limits.[3] They are widely seen as conditioning when the use of the state's coercive force is legitimate. In view of these facts, the judicial powers of the European Court of Human Rights are normatively governed by the value of legality, ie the value that sets the conditions under which state coercion is legitimate.

These facts distinguish the ECHR from other international human rights treaties towards which the relevant actors (states, individuals, and courts) need not have this attitude. It is therefore no surprise that, as we shall see, there has been great concern with how the European Court of Human Rights uses its powers of interpretation, including calls for judicial restraint and accusations of illegitimate judicial discretion. One finds in the literature on the ECtHR the same controversies and disagreements that have surrounded the role of the United States Supreme Court for decades that one would be highly unlikely to find in any international human rights monitoring body.

Recall the argument that the value of legality requires the state to govern through a coherent set of political principles whose benefit it extends to all citizens. This requirement makes what the law is on any issue a normative question, about which moral principles past political decisions entail or presuppose by way of justification.[4] Legality insists that when judges try to discover which moral principles are presupposed by past political decisions (in the case of the ECHR, states' political decision to be bound by the Convention), they operate within the law rather than exercise illegitimate judicial discretion. The only question is whether they get these moral principles right.

This chapter will begin to explore the interpretive methods used by the European Court of Human Rights, starting with autonomous concepts. The first aim of this chapter is to substantiate the claim that the practice of the ECHR is interpretive in the sense that it triggers the requirements of

---

[3] These are modifications of what Dworkin calls the 'interpretive attitude'. This attitude exists in practices that have two main characteristics: first, the practice does not simply exist but it is considered to have value that can be stated independently of describing the rules that make up the practice; and, secondly, the requirements of the practice are considered to be sensitive to its value. See *Law's Empire*, pp 46ff.

[4] See the discussion of Dworkin's idea of integrity in ch 1.

the value of legality. This rests on two propositions. First, that the Convention is widely seen as granting legal rights that condition the deploying of states' monopoly of coercive force, even when it is controversial what these rights are and institutional actors disagree. Secondly, that the relevant actors understand the ECHR rights in a non-conventionalist way: these rights need not be the same as what the Contracting States (or the majorities in them) take them to be; rather their basis is some substantive moral principle that justifies them and calls for consistent application. The case law on autonomous concepts provides an excellent example from the Court's case law in this respect.

The second aim of the chapter is to explain why disagreement about the ECHR does not necessarily entail illegitimate judicial discretion, an objection often raised against the Court's reasoning. This will clear the way for looking at the main methods of interpretation used by the European Court of Human Rights (living instrument and margin of appreciation) and for highlighting the moral principles that underpin the Convention rights and should govern their interpretation.

The Emergence of Autonomous Concepts

In 1971, Cornelis Engel and four other conscript soldiers serving in the Netherlands armed forces lodged an application with the ECtHR, claiming a violation in the imposition of penalties by military courts for disciplinary offences.[5] The applicants complained, amongst other things, that the penalties imposed on them constituted deprivation of liberty contrary to art 5 ECHR (right to liberty and security) and that the proceedings before the military authorities did not satisfy the requirements of art 6 (right to fair trial). Art 6 ECHR reads as follows: 'In the determination of his civil rights and obligations or of any criminal charge against him, everyone is entitled to a fair and public hearing within a reasonable time by an independent and impartial tribunal established by law'.

The government of the Netherlands responded that there had been no violation of art 6, because the proceedings against the applicants involved the determination neither of 'civil rights and obligations' nor of 'any criminal charge' as the above article requires. The government argued that under Netherlands law, such military penalties constituted strictly disciplinary, and not criminal, offences and that therefore art 6 of the ECHR was not at all applicable. In its judgment, the ECtHR accepted that the distinction between disciplinary proceedings and criminal proceedings was sound and reflected a long-standing practice in all the Contracting States. This practice

---

[5] *Engel and Others v the Netherlands*, Judgment of 8 June 1976, Series A no 22.

involved the distinctive character of disciplinary sentences as against criminal offences. The former were less severe, did not appear in the person's criminal record, and entailed more limited consequences than the latter. The Court, in other words, acknowledged that there were two distinct concepts in the legal practice of all Contracting States: the concept of 'disciplinary charge' and the concept of 'criminal charge'. The existence and distinctness of these two concepts was well established by reference to domestic legislation. The concept 'disciplinary charge' was introduced in laws distinct from those featuring the concept 'criminal charge' and, albeit similar in many respects, each concept was to cover different situations and to bring about different legal consequences.

Given the distinctness of the two concepts in domestic legislation, it is natural to assume, as the respondent state did, that the guarantees of art 6 do not extend to disciplinary charges but are limited to criminal charges and the 'determination of civil rights and obligations'. Yet the Court took issue with this assumption. It asked: 'Does Article 6 cease to be applicable just because the competent organs of a Contracting State classify as disciplinary an act or omission and the proceedings it takes against the author, or does it, on the contrary, apply in certain cases notwithstanding this classification?'[6]

The crucial word in the passage just quoted is 'classify'. The Court expressed the fear that some acts or omissions may be classified by the Contracting State (either intentionally, or by oversight)[7] as disciplinary offences in a way that escapes the guarantees of art 6. A few paragraphs later, the Court better explained this fear: 'If the Contracting Parties were able at their discretion to classify an offence as disciplinary instead of criminal . . . the operation of the fundamental clauses of arts 6 and 7 would be subordinated to their sovereign will'. The Court found this fear to be a legitimate one according to the provisions of the Convention, something that if tolerated would lead to 'results incompatible with the purpose and object of the Convention'.

As a means to prevent contracting states from circumventing the Convention guarantees in this way, the Court employed a solution previously developed by the European Commission in some of its first resolutions. The solution is what I shall call, following the Court, the *theory of autonomous concepts*. What exactly is this theory?

---

[6] ibid para 80.

[7] The Court does not explain whether the classification is made with the specific intention to circumvent the Convention guarantees, or the circumvention is a mere consequence of such a classification. It does imply though that this distinction is not important. What matters is whether the Convention guarantees have been circumvented as matters of fact, regardless of whether States intended so.

In one of the first characterizations of autonomous concepts, the Commission noted that the Convention terms 'criminal charge', and 'civil rights and obligations':

cannot be construed as a mere reference to the domestic law of the High Contracting Party concerned but relate to an autonomous concept which must be interpreted independently, even though the general principles of the High Contracting Parties must necessarily be taken into consideration in any such interpretation.[8]

The idea behind this passage implies a certain asymmetry or tension: on the one hand, the concepts of the Convention, and on the other hand, the meaning that these concepts have in domestic law. The Commission granted that there is a lack of correspondence between the two and it made a claim about their relation: domestic law classification is relevant but not decisive for the meaning of the concepts of the Convention. This is what the adjective 'autonomous' stands for: the autonomous concepts of the Convention enjoy a status of semantic independence—their meaning is not to be equated with the meaning that these very same concepts possess in domestic law. In other words, 'ECHR criminal charge' does not necessarily mean 'domestic-law criminal charge'.

The Court made use of the theory of autonomous concepts in *Engel* to counter the possibility of what it took to be a circumvention of the Convention guarantees. In order to do this, the Court conceded the possibility of an asymmetry between the Convention and domestic meaning: what the respondent state's law means by 'criminal charge' and 'disciplinary charge' is not the same as what the Convention means by the same terms. This enabled the Court to examine whether a situation that the respondent state classifies as a 'disciplinary offence' might turn out to be a 'criminal offence' thus demanding higher protection: 'The Court therefore...has jurisdiction to satisfy itself that the disciplinary does not improperly encroach upon the criminal'.[9] If there is such encroachment, then the Court took itself to be under an obligation to find a violation, despite the fact that, in Netherlands law, military offences are not considered to be criminal.

Since the *Engel* case, the Court has developed the theory of autonomous concepts to make it a significant doctrine of its jurisprudence. The Court and the former Commission have so far characterized as autonomous a significant number of concepts that figure in the Convention: *criminal charge*,[10]

---

[8] *Twenty-One Detained Persons v Germany*, EComHR, Decision of 6 April 1968, Collection 27 (at 97–116), para 4.

[9] *Engel*, para 81.

[10] *Demicoli v Malta*, Judgment of 28 August 1991, Series A no 210; *Özturk v Germany*, Judgment of 21 February 1984, Series A no 73; *Campbell and Fell v United Kingdom*, Judgment of 28 June 1984, Series A no 80; *Ravnsborg v Sweden*, Judgment of 23 March 1992, Series A no 283-B.

civil rights and obligations,[11] *possessions*,[12] *association*,[13] *victim*,[14] *civil servant*,[15] *lawful detention*,[16] *home*.[17] In its most recent decisions, almost 30 years after *Engel*, the Court qualified autonomous concepts as those whose 'definition in national law has only relative value and constitutes no more than a starting point'[18] and that 'must be interpreted as having an autonomous meaning in the context of the Convention and not on the basis of their meaning in domestic law'.[19]

Good-Faith Violations of the ECHR

There is something distinctive about the human rights violation that occurs in autonomous concepts. For at first sight, the state appears to have provided in its legislation all the relevant guarantees, in terms of securing the enabling conditions for the exercise of the right. Take for example the right to fair trial that was the issue in the *Engel* case. Like any other right institutionally guaranteed, protection has to do with all the state acts and omissions that are necessary for securing it: inform the accused person promptly, give him adequate time for the preparation of his defence, provide him with legal assistance, allow the examination of witnesses and the like. Such acts or omissions are enabling conditions for the exercise of the right or ways of respecting that right. Every failure by the state to meet these conditions will constitute a violation of the corresponding right. Many of these enabling conditions for

---

[11] *X v Germany*, EComHR, Decision of 21 March 1972, Collection 40, at 11–14; *Konig v Germany*, Judgment of 28 June 1978, Series A no 27; *Sporrong and Lonnroth v Sweden*, Judgment of 23 September 1982, Series A no 52; *F v United Kingdom*, Decision of 28 July 1986, unreported; *University of Illinois Foundation v Netherlands*, Decision of 2 May 1988, unreported; *B v Netherlands*, Decision of 14 July 1988, unreported.

[12] *Gasus Dosier und Fordertechnik GmbH v Netherlands*, Judgment of 23 February 1995, Series A no 306-B; *Pressos Compania Navera SA and Others v Belgium*, Judgment of 20 November 1995, Series A no 332; *Matos e Silva Lda and Others v Portugal*, Judgment of 16 September 1996, Reports 1996-IV; *Iatridis v Greece*, Judgment of 25 March 1999, Reports 1999-II; *Beyeler v Italy*, Judgment of 5 January 2000, Reports 2000-I; *Former King of Greece v Greece*, Judgment of 23 November 2000, Reports 2000-XII.

[13] *Djavit An v Turkey*, EComHR, Decision of 14 April 1998, unreported; *Chassagnou and Others v France* (1999) 29 EHRR 615; *Karakurt v Austria*, Decision of 14 September 1999, unreported.

[14] *Asselbourg and 78 Others and Greenpeace Association-Luxembourg v Luxembourg*, Decision of 29 June 1999, Reports 1999-VI.

[15] *Pellegrin v France*, Judgment of 8 December 1999, Reports 1999-VIII; *Frydlender v France*, Judgment of 27 June 2000, Reports 2000-VII.

[16] *Eriksen v Norway*, Judgment of 27 May 1997, Reports 1997-III; *Jeznach v Poland*, Judgment of 14 December 1999, unreported; *Witold Litwa v Poland*, Judgment of 4 April 2000, Reports 2000-III.

[17] *Khatun and 180 Others v United Kingdom*, EComHR, Decision of 1 July 1998, unreported.

[18] *Chassagnou and Others v France* (1999), at para 100; *Karakurt v Austria* (1999), at 4.

[19] *RL v Netherlands*, EComHR, Decision of 18 March 1995, unreported.

the exercise of a right, however, take the form of legislation. This is notably the case in art 6: rights of the accused person operate within an institutional framework of courts and tribunals and enjoyment of the right requires granting several sub-rights through the enactment of relevant legislation. Absence of this legislation constitutes a violation under the ECHR.

Now in *Engel*, all of the above considerations appear initially to have been met as there was relevant legislation granting the right of fair trial to persons charged with criminal charges. It appeared, that is, that under Netherlands law, all persons faced with a criminal charge had the right to fair trial. The question therefore was certainly not whether the Netherlands had relevant legislation granting the right or whether Dutch courts applied existing legislation that grants this right.[20] Rather, the problem arose at the level of the scope of national legislation: the state had authoritatively qualified a Convention concept such that some instances of it were explicitly excluded from its extension,[21] even though they should not have been, in the Court's opinion. By the term 'authoritative' here, I mean that the classification was made in the legal sources of this country (statutes, Constitution, decrees, etc) and applied to the applicant's case. There was a law in the Netherlands classifying military offences as disciplinary and a judicially confirmed understanding that disciplinary offences are a distinct type of offences, separate from criminal ones. This reasoning was invoked in Engel's case and was decisive in the national courts' decisions to deny the applicant a right he claimed to have under law. Moreover, these classifications and understandings were not the product of a bad-faith attempt to deprive a group of citizens of their right to fair trial. Disciplinary offences do exist and they need not attract the guarantees of art 6 ECHR. The question was whether military offences were disciplinary.

We may summarize the violation in autonomous concepts as follows:

1. The state appears to have provided, in its legislation, all the necessary guarantees for the protection of a right to X.
2. The state has, in its legislation or judicial decisions, authoritatively defined or qualified the meaning of X by classifying some of its instances.

---

[20] Not that the latter, namely, not enforcing domestic legislation, raises an issue under the ECHR. It does not fall within the jurisdiction of the ECtHR to rule, in a direct way, whether domestic law has been violated. It does so indirectly when examining whether a state's interference with a Convention was 'prescribed by law'.

[21] I here follow loosely the distinction between intension and extension, or sense and reference, as it was first drawn by Gottlob Frege in his 'On Sense and Reference' in Geach P, Black M (eds) *Translations from the Philosophical Writings of Gottlob Frege* (1980). Intension or sense is the meaning associated with a concept, ie its semantic content, its relation with other concepts, etc. Extension or reference is the object, person, or situation in the world to which the concept uniquely applies. Note, however, that I am not also accepting Frege's view that sense determines reference. In fact, the theory of autonomous concepts is a refutation of that view.

3. The classification excludes from the extension of the concept X, some instances that in the Court's opinion, do belong to it.
4. The instances excluded do not enjoy the requisite protection by the state, as do the instances that remain within the concept's extension.
5. The status of some individuals, who were involved in the excluded instances, has been practically affected.[22]
6. These individuals claim a violation by challenging the rationale behind the classification.
7. The Court finds a violation of the right to X.

There are some interesting features in this type of violation which distinguish it from other cases of human rights violations. First, it has a semantic dimension: the applicants claim a violation by disputing the meaning that the state has assigned to a legal concept.[23] Secondly, it is indirect: although the state takes itself to have provided all the necessary guarantees for the protection of a right, it turns out that it did not do so for all required cases. These two ideas suggest that the European Court is willing indirectly to review national legislation with a view to spot good-faith errors regarding the way in which the Convention rights are affected by national legislation.[24]

More specifically, the human rights violation in autonomous concepts has four very important aspects, which I would like to highlight. The first is the *fallibility* of state classifications. In the Court's reasoning, it is possible for a state to go wrong in identifying an instance of a Convention concept, despite the fact that this identification is officially made in some piece of legislation and is traditionally accepted and confirmed by the judiciary of the country. The Netherlands, for example, was wrong to classify criminal offences as not covering military offences. In fact, the Court makes the even stronger claim that the meaning of these concepts should not be subordinated to the

---

[22] I am grateful to Nicholas Hatzis for pointing out to me that for the ECtHR to declare a violation, it is not enough that a state classification was mistaken. It must also be the case that some individual's status has been affected as a result. Note, however, that the European Court has held that actual harm is not always necessary for the finding of a violation. In some cases it ruled that the mere existence of legislation that is contrary to the ECHR violates someone's right, even if it is not enforced. See above all the case *Modinos v Cyprus* (1993) 16 EHRR 485.

[23] Strictly speaking, they are disputing a particular extension of the concept, by arguing that official understanding does not determine the legal concept's reference. But I take it that this too is a semantic view, generally speaking. See Stavropoulos N, *Objectivity in Law* (1996), at ch 2.

[24] The European Court used to note that it does not examine in abstract whether national legislation violates the ECHR but rather, whether the application of national legislation to the applicant's case amounts to a violation. This is reminiscent of the distinction between 'as-applied' and 'facial challenges' to legislation in the context of the US Supreme Court adjudication. See the discussion in Fallon R, 'As-Applied and Facial Challenges and Third-Party Standing' 113 *Harvard Law Review* (2000) 1321. After the introduction of the device pilot-judgment, it is difficult to resist the claim that the European Court is ruling on the compatibility of national legislation with the ECHR.

states' 'sovereign will'. This latter remark certainly implies that these concepts should not be understood in a conventionalist sense, by looking at how most officials apply them. Their meaning may transcend what most people in the respondent state think or how officials classify the concept. Judge Van Dijk has eloquently captured this idea behind autonomous concepts in a dissenting opinion concerning the meaning of sex under art 8 ECHR: 'I cannot see any reason why legal recognition of reassignment of sex requires that biologically there has also been a (complete) reassignment; the law can give an *autonomous meaning* to the concept of "sex", as it does to concepts like "person", "family", "home", "property", etc'.[25] 'Autonomous meaning' is here linked directly to the idea that the Convention concepts should not be interpreted in a conventionalist way.

The second aspect of the human rights violation in autonomous concepts is the fact the applicant directs her challenge against domestic classifications. The applicant does not argue directly that her rights have been violated but is first interested in disputing the correctness of some official classification. She takes it to be the case that unless the classification is mistaken, she enjoys no right under the ECHR and that the finding of a violation turns on the intelligibility and success of challenging domestic classification.

Thirdly, the challenge is not austere, simply stating the facts and arguing that the right to fair trial should be granted. Rather, it is supported by arguments about what really counts as an instance of the relevant legal concept, not only in the applicant's case, but more broadly speaking. It is an argument about what should count as a criminal charge in general, for the purposes of the right to fair trial under art 6 ECHR.

The fourth and final point is the *interdependence* between the ECHR concepts and domestic legislation. The ECtHR does not take the concept that figures in domestic legislation to be coextensive with the one in the Convention (there is scope for error), but it does not take it to be totally irrelevant either. Emphasis is put on the fact that domestic use of that concept is a 'starting point'. There is, in other words, a kind of *dialogue* between national courts and legislatures on one hand, and the European Court on the other.

A More Recent Example of an Autonomous Concept

Let me provide another example of an autonomous concepts case to shape and sharpen the above remarks. In a more recent case, *Chassagnou v France* (1999), the applicants complained that compulsory membership in the Approved Municipal Hunters' Association (Associations Communales de Chasse Agréées—'ACCAs'),

---

[25] Judge Van Dijk dissenting in *Sheffield and Horsham v United Kingdom*, Judgment of 30 July 1998, Reports 1998-V (emphasis added).

violated their freedom of association under art 11 of the Convention. The applicants had been obliged, despite their ethical opposition to hunting, to transfer hunting rights over their land to the ACCAs and automatically become members of these associations. The applicants claimed a violation of their freedom of association by appealing to the well-established feature of some human rights, that a substantive part of the freedom is its negative side *not* to exercise an aspect of the right, if one does not want to. Consequently, compulsory membership to any association violates this particular aspect of the right, namely the freedom not to participate in any association whatsoever.

The respondent state did not question this latter argument at all. It did not try to argue, for example, that compulsory membership in this case is a legitimate limitation of freedom of association because of some outweighing public interest. Rather, it argued that in French law, the ACCAs were not associations *at all*, and thus no question of a violation *could* arise. More concretely France argued that ACCAs 'were public-law para-administrative institutions whose internal governing bodies admittedly resembled those of associations, but whose constitution clearly distinguished them from ordinary associations'. The respondent government insisted that public law or 'para-administrative' institutions do not fall within the meaning of an 'association', the former being subject to public law and the latter having an exclusively private character. Thus, the respondent state concluded that in the present case the right to association had no application and consequently there could be no violation.

The applicants disagreed with this line of reasoning. They provided substantive arguments to the effect that a hunters' association, even though approved by the public authorities, remained a purely private-law body. They pointed to the fact that it was presided over by a hunter who was elected by hunters, that they were not vested with any public-authority prerogative outside the scope of the ordinary law, and that the technique of official approval was not sufficient to transform a private-law association into a public administrative body—other things being equal.

The Court conceded that the applicants' point is reasonable and that the respondent government's argument is beside the point. Applying the theory of autonomous concepts to the case, it observed that *"the question is not so much whether in French law ACCAs are private associations, public or para-public associations, or mixed associations, but whether they are associations for the purposes of Article 11 of the Convention"*.[26] It furthermore reaffirmed the rationale behind the theory of autonomous concepts:

If Contracting States were able, at their discretion, by classifying an association as 'public' or 'para-administrative', to remove it from the scope of Article 11, that would give

---

[26] *Chassagnou,* para 100 (emphasis added).

them such latitude that it might lead to results incompatible with the object and purpose of the Convention, which is to protect rights that are not theoretical or illusory but practical and effective... The term 'association' therefore possesses an *autonomous meaning*; the classification in national law has only relative value and constitutes no more than a starting-point.[27]

Autonomous Concepts and Judicial Discretion

How is the autonomy of the Convention concepts from the domestic ones to be explained? How, if at all, is it possible on the Court's view that the state could make a *mistake* on what a criminal charge is? After all, many of the concepts that the Court dubs as autonomous are distinctively *legal* concepts: they are technical terms that are employed in national legal sources and are invested with a special, non-ordinary, meaning. In fact, they often gain their meaning as a result of an authoritative stipulation: what is a criminal charge and what is not, solely depends on how the relevant concept is used in legal sources. 'Criminal charge' is not like an everyday, layman's concept but it gains, as it were, its full life and meaning within law's eccentric vocabulary. Is it not the case that the only meaning these concepts can have is the one conventionally recognized by domestic law?

Justice Matscher, one of the former ECtHR judges, has been a critic of the theory of autonomous concepts from the very beginning. He writes for example:

Even if it is necessary, for purposes of autonomous qualification of a concept in an international convention, to depart from the formal qualification given to an institution in the legislation of a given State and to analyse its real nature, this process must never go too far—otherwise there is a danger of arriving at an abstract qualification which may be philosophically valid, but which has no basis in law.[28]

Matscher's objection is premised on the view that every deviation from domestic classification carries the danger of going beyond law's boundaries, ie beyond what the law *is*. The danger involves going as far as creating a new, extra-legal concept that has little or nothing to do with the legal one. This danger, if true, would of course pose a serious threat to the theory of autonomous concepts. For the judges' task is to apply what the law *is*, not to say what the law *should* be. This is a fundamental principle of the rule of law: we should regret if judges legislate retroactively, ie if they have the discretion to create a new legal duty or right, based on what they think the law should be, while existing law is quite different on the matter. The sceptical

[27] ibid (emphasis added).
[28] Dissenting Opinion of Judge Matscher in *Özturk v Germany* (1984).

challenge to autonomous concepts seems to raise an objection of illegitimate judicial discretion: going beyond what is accepted in domestic law and seeking abstract theorizations of the ECHR rights amounts to extending the law and amending the Convention.

Do autonomous concepts constitute a case of illegitimate judicial legislation? Do European Court judges usurp their power by seeking an 'abstract qualification which may be philosophically valid but which has no basis in law', as Judge Matscher vividly puts it?

Need for Harmonization and Uniform Application?

Suppose we try to justify the use of autonomous concepts on the grounds that they are necessary in every multilateral treaty. Imagine the argument going as follows. 'There is nothing special about autonomous concepts cases; they are just the result of the fact that Strasbourg adjudicates on cases coming from different jurisdictions, the ECHR being an international convention. Departure from domestic definitions may not only be acceptable, but also necessary for international instruments whose main aim is to coordinate different legal systems. Although the Contracting Parties had to share some legal concepts in order to draft the Convention in the first place, we should expect that there are still important differences as to how these concepts are understood and classified in each domestic law. Hence, since conformity to the classification of one state's domestic law would only constitute a violation of the classification of some other state's domestic law, departure from domestic definitions is unavoidable. The Court, on this account, must necessarily have some *discretion* to legislate in these borderline cases and secure the harmonization of national laws.' Call this the international theorist's argument.

Pointing to this aspect of the ECHR as a way to explain the need for autonomous concepts looks indeed a very powerful suggestion. The idea seems to run as follows. The Contracting States roughly share, in their legal system, the same legal concepts. This is a natural prerequisite, for otherwise, how did they come together and agree on the same text? However, in interpreting these legal concepts, there are bound to be borderline *differences* as to how the various legal systems understand and qualify these concepts. What for Netherlands law is a disciplinary offence may constitute a criminal offence for German or English law. What for French law is a para-administrative institution may be a private association for Greek or Italian law. In other words, states do not always agree on what an association or a criminal charge is; they do not always speak, as it were, 'the same language'—both literally and metaphorically. They may classify some situations differently, which means that domestic legislations *diverge* on whether some instance (say a hunters' union in the *Chassagnou* case) falls below the same legal concept (association). European Court judges must then exercise a power of discretion to fill in the gaps created by border-line discrepancies among Contracting States with a view to achieve uniform application of the Convention across states.

The international theorist's explanation, however, may be valid for other multilateral treaties (like the EC) which aim at coordination, but it cannot fully explain the presence of autonomous concepts in the ECHR. This is so because all the characteristics of autonomous concepts that I earlier pointed out have nothing to do with some alleged divergence among Contracting States or the need for coordination. The Court concedes that the applicant is making a legitimate claim *before* considering whether the rest of the states diverge on the issue. Nor does the applicant argue his case in the way the international theorist's argument suggests. The applicant in autonomous concepts cases claims that the understanding of a legal concept that his country employs in domestic legislation does not capture what this concept amounts to within the meaning of the ECHR. He does not argue that his state's classification is problematic for the sole reason that there is no uniform understanding of this concept among Contracting States and coordination breaks down.

For suppose the international theorist's argument were valid. In this case, the applicant's argumentative challenge would have to be driven by this alleged divergence. It would go something along the following lines: I claim that my right to fair trial under the European Convention has been violated because there is no agreement among Contracting States on some particular aspect of this right which applies to my situation. Such an argument though is totally absent from the ECtHR legal practice. Nor does the ECtHR take itself to use the theory of autonomous concepts as a tool of judicial discretion in the face of divergence. It does not picture autonomous concepts as an inevitable power of discretion due to some conceptual differences among contracting legal systems that must be ironed-out. To the contrary, the Court has developed this theory to prevent Contracting States from violating the Convention guarantees, as a matter of what these legal standards have always amounted to. Recall that in autonomous concepts cases, the Court warned against circumventing the Convention guarantees, not against having exceptions to a uniform classification across the Contracting States. The aim is clearly to respect what the Convention grants and not to solve some alleged problem of divergence or coordination. The Court in *Engel* and *Chassagnou* declared a violation and held Contracting States accountable on the basis that the applicant had been denied a right which is embodied in the Convention, not on the basis that, absent a uniform understanding of the concept, the Convention grants no such right and judges have discretion to grant or deny it.[29]

Autonomous Concepts as Disagreement

So it seems that mere divergence between Contracting States on how they classify concepts cannot alone explain autonomous concepts. A different approach is needed in order to explain autonomous concepts. We need to find the rationale behind the autonomy of these concepts by examining the relevance of domestic classification on one hand and the applicant's correspondent claim of violation on the other. Here is my suggestion: we can very easily redescribe this lack of convergence among national classifications as a *disagreement* between two or more individuals over the nature or character of a particular object, practice or state of affairs. Take for example the military punishment in the *Engel* case: one person, A, calls it a disciplinary offence, whereas another, B, calls it a criminal offence. That is, B insists that the law gives to people who have been charged with a military offence a right to a fair trial, whereas A thinks that the law denies them this right. Both of them argue their case as a matter of what the law allows, imposes, grants, or denies.

We do not have to personify the Contracting States for this picture to work: domestic classification is the result of real people (legislators, framers, judges, committee experts) drafting statutes, enacting laws, or taking decisions that have a bearing on these concepts' meaning. In fact, this synchronic disagreement is not that hard to imagine, for it actually takes places before the ECtHR in autonomous concepts cases. Recall that in these cases the applicant disputes his own state's classification of a concept and puts forward a different understanding of it, while the state insists that the applicant's conception is wrong. More importantly, the applicant *knows* that in his state, military offences are not considered criminal, yet disagrees that this classification is correct, as a matter of *law*, ie as a matter of what the ECHR entitles people to.

To use a different vocabulary, applicants propose a different *conception* of what *counts* as an instance of a legal concept, say criminal charge.[30] In *Engel* the state relied on a conception according to which disciplinary offences are not criminal, whereas the applicants' and the Court's conception was such

---

[29] The only alternative left here would be to argue that judges and applicants are partners to an institutional fraud: they are both lying about the reasons they use to back up their legal arguments. I take it that this extravagant view would be even harder to swallow in the case of a court as important as the ECtHR. What reason would judges in Strasbourg have to hide, in a joint and continuous conspiracy, their preference for judicial legislation behind the theory of autonomous concepts?

[30] The *locus classicus* of this distinction is Rawls J, *A Theory of Justice* (1999 revised edn), at 5 and Dworkin R, *Law's Empire*, at 90.

that they are. Given that the ECHR provides protection for criminal offences alone, there is an open question of which conception of this concept is the correct one for the purposes of the ECHR. It is not at all accidental that the Court terms these Convention concepts 'autonomous' and not totally *different* concepts from the domestic ones. For the fact that the translated domestic concepts bear the same name as the Convention ones would not normally guarantee that they are all the same concepts. The Court however said explicitly that, although the state classification is not decisive, it is still *relevant*, and this can only be the case if it is still an understanding of the same concept, rather than an altogether different notion.

Seeing the matter in terms of disagreement also helps to understand better the initial suggestion that domestic legislations diverge on how they classify concepts. This idea of legal disagreement, ie disagreement over what the legal concepts mean and consequently what the law requires, is the best way to describe divergence between states. For even though it is an apparent fact that domestic legislations very often diverge on how they classify legal concepts, it is equally obvious *that they diverge on the same concepts.* Unlike some philosophical views on the matter,[31] neither the Court nor lawyers and litigants think that Contracting States have different concepts rather than different conceptions of the same concept. Everybody understands that states share the same legal concepts even though they have different and competing understandings of them. It is precisely because we often take these various classifications among states to conflict, that it makes sense to say that they are different understandings of the same *thing*, rather than different and incommensurable conceptual schemes. We do not say for instance, that in France, apart from associations, they have something called para-administrative institutions. Rather, we say that in France, unlike other countries, they do not think that hunters' unions are associations.

Autonomous concepts therefore portray vividly some challenging features of legal disagreement at the international level. First, it may be the case that the legally correct meaning of an ECHR concept may significantly depart from the one used and accepted within the national legal order. We may cast this in a more philosophical vocabulary by saying that legal truth *transcends* communal understanding and acceptance. The applicant disagrees with a conception that builds on a piece of national legislation and has been confirmed and supported by the judiciary of the country. Recall that normally the applicant is required

---

[31] There is an argument, traditionally associated with what Wittgenstein writes in *Philosophical Investigations*, in which there is no difference between following an interpretation of a certain concept and following a totally different concept. This tradition is largely due to Saul Kripke's seminal reading of Wittgenstein in Kripke S, *Wittgenstein on Rules and Private Language: an elementary exposition* (1982).

to have exhausted domestic remedies, which secures that the state's judicial authorities have already ruled that the problematic classification captures precisely the way this concept is understood in that legal community. The applicant's challenge amounts to the claim that both the courts and the legislature of that state, even the whole community of officials, may have been wrong about the classification. Disagreement, in other words, builds on the idea that the standard of legal correctness may radically transcend the applicant's legal community. The institutional loneliness of the applicant's situation thus marks the *depth* of disagreement. Persistence in the possibility of communal error within the national legal community is the driving force of the applicant's challenge.

Secondly, since there is usually divergence among Contracting States on how they classify the relevant concept, the applicant's challenge will necessarily target those as well; it will be compatible with some but incompatible with others and disagreement will potentially become explicit if applicants from other countries decide too to go to Strasbourg. Disagreement is therefore *widespread*. We should expect that legal practitioners (litigants, legislators, judges) hold and propose different understandings of legal concepts not only *within* the same legal order, ie vertically (applicant against his or her state) but also across *all* legal communities that are parties to the Convention, ie horizontally.

Does Disagreement Entail Judicial Discretion?

I said earlier that applicants propose a different conception of what counts as an instance of a legal concept, say a criminal charge. In *Engel* the state had a conception according to which disciplinary offences are not criminal, whereas the applicants' and the Court's conception was such that they are. Given that the ECHR provides protection for criminal offences alone, there is an open question as to which conception is the correct one under the law of the ECHR. But is there such a thing as a right answer in law when reasonable people disagree? Doesn't disagreement entail the lack of a right answer as a matter of law?

Recall the applicant's challenge in autonomous concepts. First, the applicant makes an issue out of how a certain situation is classified under domestic law. Applicants in autonomous concepts cases have the belief that it is important whether you call something one way or another and provide reasons why a certain classification is mistaken. Secondly, the applicant's challenge makes perfect sense within our legal practice. A litigant who argues that military proceedings are criminal rather than disciplinary makes both an interesting and intelligible claim. Legal practice is reflective enough to allow such challenges without considering them inappropriate. Consider moreover the consequences that would follow once the disagreement is resolved one way or another. If we choose to call military proceedings disciplinary, *Engel* has no right to fair trial. If instead we choose to call them criminal, the right is granted. Disagreement therefore operates on the background assumption that such classifications are not neutral because they have a direct impact on what rights people have and how state coercion will be used. Litigants who disagree on whether a hunters' union is an association, disagree at the same time about what a particular legal practice grants people. In fact it is plausible to say that they would not be having this disagreement had it not been for the fact that legal rights are at stake.

Disagreement indicates that legal practice is interpretive and that the concept of law is 'deep'. For outside law, sensible people do not disagree over whether military offences are criminal, unless they are lexicographers. We disagree about legal concepts such as the concept of a 'criminal charge' because we are particularly sensitive about what legal rights people have. Needless to say, it makes a huge difference to people if the law requires or grants something than if it does not. Disagreement in autonomous concepts is, above all, disagreement about what the European Convention entitles people as a matter of law.

Note further how the answer we give to whether military offences are criminal or disciplinary takes a stance on the point and purpose of the ECHR. If the ECtHR were to call them disciplinary, this would mean that the Convention only grants the right to fair trial to whatever each Member State understands as a criminal offence. If, on the other hand, the ECtHR were to call them criminal, this would mean that domestic classifications are not decisive and that the Court should take other principles into account when addressing the applicant's challenge. Here is a list of the questions that depend on how we would classify military offences in *Engel*:

1. Does the law of the ECHR give people charged with military offences the human right to fair trial?
2. Should the ECtHR respect domestic classifications?
3. Should ECtHR judges try to interpret and apply the ECHR according to the best moral theory of human rights?
4. Should international judges decide controversial matters that affect national governments?

Now consider the objection from judicial discretion that was raised by Judge Matscher. His objection was centred on the idea that 'departure from the formal qualification given to an institution in the legislation of a given state' and 'analysis of its real nature' carries the danger of going beyond law. This idea now seems to be beside the point. For once the situation is put in terms of disagreement over the point and purpose of the ECHR, we can see that the objection from judicial discretion actually takes sides between competing conceptions of the ECHR and the role of judges more generally. If we concede the objection and do not depart from domestic classification we would be taking sides on all the above questions. We would assume that the law of the ECHR should respect domestic classifications. We would assume the ECHR does not grant people charged with military offences the human right to a fair trial. And we would assume that judges are not supposed to interpret and apply the ECHR according to the best moral theory of human rights.

But what would be the argument for making these assumptions? The argument cannot be that the law of the ECHR requires judges to make these assumptions if they are to avoid judicial legislation. For the other side argues, very intelligibly, that the law of the ECHR requires judges to *reject* these assumptions. Accepting Judge Matscher's objection from judicial discretion, without further argument, would therefore beg the question. There is disagreement between two sides over what the law of the ECHR is and we are told to choose one side on the grounds that this is what the law of the ECHR is. In other words, the objection from judicial discretion assumes what needs to be proved. Once the picture of disagreement is revealed, the objection from judicial discretion is idle. It is clear that we need a reason why the judges of the ECtHR should privilege one conception over another. But this reason cannot be, if we do not want to beg the question, that this is what the law of the ECHR demands.

This point is extremely valuable. Judge Matscher's objection from judicial discretion was initially raised against exercising choice in interpretation. The objection was that if judges did not support the state classification, if they exercised choice by trying to find the philosophically correct meaning of the autonomous concept, then they would be making new law. But now we see that such judicial inertness amounts to a full-blooded choice, as we might put it. Legal disagreement makes it the case that no matter what judges do, they will still be exercising choice in the sense of privileging one conception of the ECHR over the other. It is because of legal disagreement that judges must necessarily make choices in interpretation rather than open-texture, vagueness,[32] or divergence among Contracting States.

---

[32] I do not face vagueness head-on as a possible source of indeterminacy and discretion, independently of that of substantive disagreement. Timothy Endicott explores this issue in Endicott T, *Vagueness in Law* (2000). It is, to be sure, logically possible that some concepts or issues are vague even if people do not bother to disagree about them. In this sense, vagueness is independent from disagreement. But to the extent that vagueness becomes relevant to legal adjudication, we should expect that litigants put forth substantive arguments, similar to the ones in autonomous concepts, to counter vagueness one way or the other. In this case, we might say either that litigants try to

Possible Choices

I proposed a theory for explaining autonomous concepts and argued that it unmasks broader jurisprudential truths about the entire Convention. I have said however nothing about how the underlying disagreement is to be resolved. What could count as a reason why judges should choose one conception over the other? What could count as a justification for the way judges are to resolve disagreement? For plainly, there are numerous possible ways to go about it and the justification we are seeking must be capable of choosing amongst them. Consider the following possibilities in *Engel*:

1. The ECHR grants the right to fair trial to whatever the respondent state classifies as a criminal charge.
2. The ECHR grants the right to fair trial to whatever *most* Contracting States classify as a criminal charge.
3. The ECHR grants the right to fair trial to whatever is the morally best conception of what counts as a criminal charge, even if no one actually holds it or no piece of national legislation or case law expresses it.
4. The ECHR grants the right to fair trial to whatever is the morally best conception of what counts as a criminal charge, as long as at this conception is expressed in some piece of national legislation or case law.
5. The ECHR grants the right to fair trial to whatever is the morally best conception of what counts as a criminal charge even if it is not expressed in any legislation, as long as at least some *people* in the societies of the contracting states hold it.
6. The ECHR grants the right to fair trial to whatever situations the drafters thought or would have wanted or expected to apply.
7. At the face of disagreement, the ECHR does not grant the right to fair trial. The matter should be left to each Contracting State to decide whether military proceedings are criminal.

While not exhaustive, the list that the interpretation of the Convention faces is a rich set of choices, all of which have a bearing on what legal rights people have, and is a set much richer in fact than the one the judicial discretion-by-default thesis worried about. As we saw, none of these choices may be discounted on the question-begging grounds that it goes beyond law's limits. The situation is such that judges need to make a choice in order to find what the law of the ECHR is, and choices do not come easy; whichever of the seven

---

resolve some inherent conceptual vagueness or, more plausibly, *that they disagree with those that find this matter vague and indeterminate.* For clearly, vagueness is a belief people hold about concepts, not a mind-independent feature of things. Indeed, it is difficult to see how any discussion of vagueness in law can be interesting if it is not linked to the idea of substantive disagreement.

possibilities I listed judges might choose, there must be a reason why the rest were mistaken. Justification therefore must itself be rich enough to explain this.

I noted earlier that whereas the initial disagreement was over some legal concept, possible choices to resolve the disagreement turned on the broader point and purpose of the ECHR. For all the possibilities in the above list are also conceptions of the point and purpose of the ECHR. They all acknowledge that the ECHR is a human rights document that has been institutionalized and has created a legal practice that grants citizens of the Council of Europe some rights that are justiciable, but each possibility takes a different stance as to the nature, scope, and value of these rights. On some, the point of the ECHR is to grant people a set of moral rights against their state, regardless of what the practices are of that state; on others, that it is to grant only what rights each state expects or has explicitly agreed individuals should have. The answer to specific questions regarding disagreement about legal concepts necessarily engages an answer to the broader question of what is the point of the law of the ECHR? For example, if the applicant, Engel, was denied the right to fair trial on the basis that no state classifies military offences as criminal, that would mean that the ECHR only grants rights that the states have explicitly recognized. And vice versa: different theories of the point and purpose of the law of the ECHR will dictate different answers to what legal rights individuals that go to Strasbourg have. If for example, the point of the ECHR is to grant citizens a set of universal moral rights regardless of whether their state has explicitly considered and accepted all instances of these moral rights, then Engel has a claim even if no official or citizen has ever taken military offences to be criminal. 'Jurisprudence', Dworkin remarks, 'is the general part of adjudication, silent prologue to every decision of law'.[33]

One possible, and very popular, argument in favour of some of the above possibilities (such as points 2, 4, 6, and 7) is based on the idea that the interpretation of the ECHR, and international law in general, should promote certainty and should not defeat the expectations that states have formed about their treaty obligations. This argument, which goes against the idea of interpreting the ECHR rights in their best moral light and independently of states' expectations and consensus, is examined in the next chapter. As we shall see, this argument not only fails in the case of human rights but is also incompatible with the European Court's long-standing rejection of intentionalism and textualism.

---

[33] Dworkin R, *Law's Empire* (1986) at 90.

3

Intentionalism, Textualism, and Evolutive Interpretation

Of all the criticisms leveled against textualism, the most mindless is that it is 'formalistic'. The answer to that is, of course, it's formalistic! The rule of law is about form [. . .] A murderer has been caught with blood on his hands, bending over the body of his victim; a neighbour with a video camera has filmed the crime; and the murderer has confessed in writing and on videotape. We nonetheless insist that before the state can punish this miscreant, it must conduct a full-dress criminal trial that results in a verdict of guilty. Is that not formalism? Long live formalism. It is what makes a government a government of laws and not of men.

Antonin Scalia[1]

'The Constitution is a written instrument. As such, its meaning does not alter. That which it meant when adopted it means now'.

Brewer J[2]

The mere fact that a body was not envisaged by the drafters of the Convention cannot prevent that body from falling within the scope of the Convention.

European Court of Human Rights[3]

Introduction

What is the connection between the interpretation of the ECHR rights and drafters' original intentions? As an international treaty, the ECHR is subject to the rules of interpretation of treaties set out in the Vienna Convention on the Law of Treaties (VCLT). Looking at the ECtHR case law one finds

---

[1] Scalia A, 'Common Law Courts in a Civil Law System' in Gutman A, (ed) *A Matter of Interpretation* (1997) at 24.
[2] *South Carolina v United States* 199 US 437, 448 (1905).
[3] *Matthews v United Kingdom*, Judgment of 18 February 1999, Reports 1999-I, para 39.

relatively few references to arts 31–33 of the VCLT.[4] Close as its methods are to the general rule of purposive interpretation under art 31 VCLT, the European Court has created its own labels for the interpretative techniques that it uses such as 'living-instrument', 'practical and effective rights', 'autonomous concepts' etc. What all these methods have in common is the rejection of the idea that the Convention rights must be interpreted in the light of what their meaning was taken to be back in the 1950s. The European Court has repeatedly stressed that the Convention is a 'living instrument' which must be interpreted 'in the light of present-day conditions'. This is in line with art 31 para 1 VCLT which prioritizes the 'object and purpose' of treaties as a general rule of interpretation and assigns to preparatory works a supplementary role. According to art 32 VCLT, recourse to supplementary means of interpretation, such as preparatory works, may be had 'in order to confirm the meaning resulting from the application of art 31, or to determine the meaning when the interpretation according to art 31: (a) leaves the meaning ambiguous or obscure; or (b) leads to a result which is manifestly absurd or unreasonable'.

Yet the connection between drafters' original intentions and 'here and now' interpretation of human rights is not one that we can easily set aside. This is evident in how influential originalist theories of interpretation have been in the context of domestic law, particularly in American constitutional law and theory. The link between drafters' intentions and judicial interpretation has always been a controversial issue in legal philosophy and it has been raised before the European Court on several occasions. This chapter addresses the European Court's approach to drafters' intentions and the VCLT in the light of this general philosophical question, in order to strengthen the claim that the correct interpretation of the ECHR rights turns on the moral principles that underpin human rights.

---

[4] Article 31 VCLT provides that: '1. A treaty shall be interpreted in good faith in accordance with the ordinary meaning to be given to the terms of the treaty in their context and in the light of its object and purpose. 2. The context for the purpose of the interpretation of a treaty shall comprise, in addition to the text, including its preamble and annexes: (a) any agreement relating to the treaty which was made between all the parties in connection with the conclusion of the treaty; (b) any instrument which was made by one or more parties in connection with the conclusion of the treaty and accepted by the other parties as an instrument related to the treaty. 3. There shall be taken into account, together with the context: (a) any subsequent agreement between the parties regarding the interpretation of the treaty or the application of its provisions; (b) any subsequent practice in the application of the treaty which establishes the agreement of the parties regarding its interpretation; (c) any relevant rules of international law applicable in the relations between the parties. 4. A special meaning shall be given to a term if it is established that the parties so intended'.

Originalism in Constitutional Law

Originalist[5] theories wish to tie interpretation back to the time when the law was enacted. We can distinguish between two types of originalism. The first one, textualism, argues that a legal provision must mean what it was taken to mean originally, ie at the time of enactment. Rather than ask ourselves, for example, whether the right not to be subjected to inhuman and degrading treatment under art 3 ECHR applies to circumstances of extreme poverty, we should ask: 'Did the public at large in 1950 understand extreme poverty to be an instance of inhuman and degrading treatment?' Textualists invite the interpreter to focus on the text enacted and read it in the light of its social and linguistic context at the time of adoption.[6] Judges must 'immerse themselves'[7] in the society that adopted the text and understand the text as they understood it then.

The second one, intentionalism, argues that a legal provision must apply to whatever cases the drafters had originally intended it to apply. Intentionalism takes legal interpretation to be a form of *conversational* interpretation. Rather than ask ourselves whether the right not to be subjected to inhuman and degrading treatment should be applied to circumstances of extreme poverty, we should ask: 'Did the drafters intend this right to apply to socio-economic conditions?' Intentionalists usually propose the following scheme: if the drafters contemplated a particular situation then they either intended to prohibit it or they did not. If they did not intend to prohibit it then they either intended not to prohibit it or they left the matter open for the courts to decide.[8] Intentionalists put more emphasis on drafting history and preparatory works as their task is to retrieve the original understanding of particular legislators.[9]

Originalism, in its various forms, has been a very influential doctrine in American constitutional law. It is held by many constitutional theorists

[5] See Bork R, *The Tempting of America* (1989) at 143–60; Scalia A, 'Originalism: The Lesser Evil' 57 *University of Cincinnati Law Review* (1989) 849–65; Scalia A, 'Common Law Courts in a Civil Law System', in Gutman A (ed) *A Matter of Interpretation* (1997) at 3–47; Gray T, 'Do We Have an Unwritten Constitution?' 27 *Stanford Law Review* (1975) 703; Lyons D, 'Constitutional Interpretation and Original Meaning' 4 *Social Philosophy and Policy* (1986) 85.

[6] Brest P, 'The Misconceived Quest for the Original Understanding' 60 *Boston University Law Review* (1980) 204, at 208.

[7] Brest, ibid.

[8] Perry MJ, 'Interpretivism, Freedom of Expression and Equal Protection' 42 *Ohio State Law Journal* (1981) 261.

[9] I should note here that textualism, at least as advanced by Scalia, is also a form of intentionalism: it directs us to the intentions of the public at the time of enactment. The difference between the two lies in the group of people, whose intentions the interpreter aims to discover: textualism is directed at the community at large whereas intentionalism is directed at the drafters. I am grateful to Aileen Kavanagh for this point.

as well as judges and it has always been a very controversial doctrine. The controversy over originalism was initiated in the 19th century as the debate over whether constitutional interpretation should be based on common law doctrinal techniques or on methods of statutory interpretation. Later on, as constitutional adjudication gradually shifted from review of economic measures to civil liberties, originalism became the favourite theory of advocates of judicial self-restraint. It was used to criticize the Supreme Court's activism during the Warren period and to offer a theory of interpretation that would prevent judges from deciding evaluative issues. Later in 1987, the discussion on the merits of originalism was reheated, when President Reagan nominated Robert Bork for the Supreme Court, a judge famous for his extreme originalist views on how to interpret constitutional rights. The issue attracted broad publicity, Bork's views were finally rejected by the Senate, and his nomination was defeated.

Golder v UK: VCLT and the Case of Unenumerated Rights

Golder[10] is undoubtedly one of the most important cases in the history of the ECHR. It is not just that it contains the first and as yet most extensive discussion of the Vienna Convention on the Law of Treaties (VCLT) and the relevant rules of interpretation. It is also the first major case in its early years where the Court had to take a stance on what should be the general theory of interpreting the Convention and the relevance of original intentions. There was, in 1975, no right of direct access to the Court and very little case law on the substantive rights of the Convention. The VCLT itself had not entered into force. Moreover none of the interpreting methods that the Court is now famous for had at the time been fully advanced. *Tyrer*,[11] which inaugurated the 'living-instrument' approach was decided in 1978. *Engel*,[12] which systematized the theory of autonomous concepts was decided in 1976 and *Airey*, which provided an extensive application of the idea of 'practical and effective rights' was decided in 1978. *Golder* laid the foundations for the interpretative principles that have now become so important for the thousands of applications that the Court receives each year.

The legal question in *Golder* was one that has fuelled the various debates between originalist and non-originalists in the context of American constitutional law, namely that of 'unenumerated' rights.[13] These are rights that

[10] *Golder v United Kingdom*, Judgment of 21 February 1975, Series A no 18.
[11] *Tyrer v United Kingdom*, Judgment of 25 April 1978, Series A no 26.
[12] *Engel and Others v Netherlands* (1976) Series A no 22.
[13] On the distinction between enumerated and unenumerated rights see Dworkin R, *Life's Dominion* (1993) at 129.

are not expressly mentioned in the text but it is proposed that they should nevertheless be 'read into' it. The right in *Golder* was that of access to court under art 6 ECHR. The applicant, a prisoner serving his sentence, had been denied permission to consult a solicitor with a view to institute libel proceedings against a prison officer. The United Kingdom, which was the respondent state, argued that the ECHR does not confer a right to access to court, given the absence of an explicit provision: if a person gets to court he must be given a fair trial, but there is no obligation on the part of the Member State to ensure that everyone gets to have his case heard. Its argument was not so much to do with the intentions of the drafters as found in preparatory works. Rather it was premised on the idea that the text itself gives a clear indication of drafters' intentions: had the drafters intended to create this right they would have done so explicitly by choosing a different wording. In support of this argument the respondent state added that the drafters had clearly thought about the right of access since it is expressly mentioned in art 5 para 4 and art 13 ECHR yet they omitted it from art 6.

In its judgment, the Court made reference to arts 31–33 of the VCLT and held that, although not yet in force, these articles enunciate general principles of international law that it has to take into account. It then first examined the language of art 6 ECHR and whether it settles the relevant legal question, namely whether the ECHR protects the right of access to court. It concluded that the language does not 'necessarily refer only to proceedings already pending' but may well imply 'the right to have the determination of disputes relating to civil rights and obligations made by a court or 'tribunal'.[14] In other words it held that the wording itself was *neutral* between these two options.

The Court then elaborated on the 'object and purpose' of the Convention, by turning to the preamble of the Convention, as provided for in art 31 para 2 of the VCLT. It cited the passage in the ECHR preamble that refers to the 'common heritage of political traditions, ideals, freedom, and the rule of law' of European countries and noted that 'in civil matters one can scarcely conceive of the rule of law without there being a possibility of having access to courts'.[15] This account of the rule of law was, on the Court's view, in accordance with a general principle of law among Contracting States whereby 'a civil claim must be capable of being submitted to a judge'.

The Court further made the hypothetical point that if the Convention did not guarantee the right to access to court, states 'could without in breach of that text, do away with courts, or take away their jurisdiction to determine certain class of civil actions and entrust it to organs dependent on the

---

[14] *Golder v United Kingdom* (1975), para 32.
[15] ibid para 34.

Government'.[16] Such assumptions, the Court held, are 'indissociable from a danger of arbitrary power' and would have serious consequences which are 'repugnant' to the principle of the rule of law. It concluded that the right of access constitutes an element which is 'inherent' in the right stated by art 6 para 1 and warned that this is not an 'extensive interpretation forcing new obligations on the Contracting States: it is based on the very terms of the first sentence of art 6 para 1 (art 6–(1)) read in its context and having regard to the object and purpose of the Convention'.[17] It added that there is no need to resort to supplementary means of interpretation as envisaged at art 32 of the VCLT.

This was an important line of reasoning. The Court not only rejected the view that lack of an explicit provision in the text constitutes an obstacle for granting an unenumerated right. It also stressed that the question whether to grant an unenumerated right is not a question of whether we should stick to the actual text or extend its meaning through interpretation. For the majority of judges in *Golder* did not think they added the right of access to court to art 6 ECHR; they insisted that by recognizing the right to access to court, they followed an interpretation based on 'the very terms' of the first sentence of art 6 para 1 and did not force any 'new' obligations on the Contracting States. On the contrary, they thought that fidelity to art 6 ECHR demanded granting this right. 'This is what the text says', they could have said, 'these are its very terms'.

But the Court did not just announce that the right of access to court was included within 'the very terms' of art 6. It gave clear reasons why it thought so. Recall the Court's line of reasoning:

1. In interpretation, one should look at the object and purpose of the law.
2. The object and purpose of the ECHR is to promote the rule of law.
3. One can scarcely conceive of the rule of law in civil matters without right of access to court.
4. The right of access to court is 'inherent' in the right to fair trial under art 6 ECHR.
5. The ECHR protects the right of access to court.

Moreover, the Court followed this reasoning without feeling the need to resort to supplementary means of interpretation such as the preparatory works. It felt confident that 'the object and purpose' of the ECHR contains the ideal of the rule of law which leaves no ambiguity (necessary for resorting to supplementary means under art 32 VCLT) as to whether it requires a right of

---

[16] ibid para 35.
[17] ibid para 36. The Court added that there was no need to resort to supplementary means of interpretation.

access to court. Although the text appeared neutral to the legal question, the question became quite clear in the light of the principle of the rule of law.

The above reasoning did not come without objections on the part of some European Court judges. In a lengthy separate opinion, Sir Gerald Fitzmaurice mounted an originalist attack on the majority judgment. He objected that it is unacceptable to read into the text a right 'which the Convention does not trouble to name, but at the most implies, and which cannot even usefully be implied without at the same time proceeding to a rather careful definition of it, or of the conditions subject to which it operates, and which, by circumscribing it, define it'.[18] Fitzmaurice followed a typical intentionalist argument: if the drafters did not clearly intend to create a right of access to court then they could not have created one.[19] In his view, lack of an express provision and detailed definition of a right of access meant that states were not bound by such a right and that the European court should not impose a new obligation on Member States by recognizing it.

Fitzmaurice's arguments in his separate opinion in *Golder* merit a more careful discussion. His intentionalist views were based on an argument about the importance of *certainty* in international law. It is important, the British judge argued, that states have knowledge of the obligations they have undertaken by signing a treaty. 'The parties', he said, 'cannot be expected to implement what would be an important international obligation when it is not defined sufficiently to enable them to know exactly what it involves'.[20] At this point Fitzmaurice drew a distinction between national and international law. Judicial legislation, he argued, may be acceptable in domestic adjudication,[21] but it is totally unacceptable in international adjudication which is based on agreement between states.[22] Even if the lack of a right of access is a regrettable defect of the ECHR—he argued in elegant call for restraint—

[i]t is for the States upon whose consent the Convention rests, and from which consent alone it derives its obligatory force, to close the gap or put the defect right by an amendment—not for a judicial tribunal to substitute itself for the convention-makers, to do their work for them.

The only case where an international tribunal would be justified in substituting itself for the Convention-makers according to Fitzmaurice is if state

---

[18] Judge Sir Gerald Fitzmaurice, separate opinion in *Golder,* para 28.

[19] See also ibid, para 40: 'It is hardly possible to establish what really were the intentions of the Contracting States under this head; but that of course is all the more reason for not subjecting them to obligations which do not result clearly from the Convention, or at least in a manner free from reasonable doubt'.

[20] ibid para 30.

[21] For a judge of a common law country, Fitzmaurice was surprisingly sceptical of the legitimacy of judge-made law in England.

[22] Recall Lord Hoffmann's similar views in *Jones v Ministry of Interior Al-Mamlaka Al-Arabiya AS Saudiya (Kingdom of Saudi Arabia) and Others* [2006] UKHL 26, para 63.

parties clearly intended to delegate this power to it. But he did not find any signs of such intention in the ECHR.

After *Golder*: the ECHR as a Living Instrument

Fitzmaurice's originalist call for judicial restraint did not persuade his fellow judges to change their interpretive methods. In a case that was decided eight months after *Golder*, the British judge continued to defend originalism against an idea that was becoming more and more popular with the European Court judges: namely, that the Convention should not be understood in terms of the intentions of the parties in 1950. This idea, he insisted, 'lacks realism and reason'.[23] Yet he could not have been more wrong. In the following 30 years or so, the European Court (and the former Commission) fully endorsed the idea that the Convention is a 'living instrument' that must be interpreted in the light of present-day conditions rather than what the drafters thought back in 1950.[24]

This method, also called evolutive or dynamic interpretation, proved neither unrealistic nor unreasonable. Over time the Court settled on the view that lack of a clear intention on the part of the drafters is simply irrelevant when considering whether to recognize a right or not. A fine example is found in *Matthews v United Kingdom*, where the issue was whether elections for the European Parliament fall within the right to vote under the ECHR:

That the Convention is a living instrument which must be interpreted in the light of present-day conditions is firmly rooted in the Court's case law ... *The mere fact that a body was not envisaged by the drafters of the Convention cannot prevent that body from falling within the scope of the Convention.*[25]

But the European Court went even further than that. It not only recognized rights that the drafters had not clearly intended to grant, but it also recognized rights that the drafters had clearly intended *not* to grant. The best example is the case of *Young, James and Webster*.[26] The case raised the issue of whether so-called 'closed shops' in Britain, ie the legal requirement that all employees of a certain class are members of a specified trade union, were compatible

---

[23] Separate Opinion in *National Union of Belgian Police v Belgium*, Judgment of 27 October 1975, para 7.

[24] See *Tyrer v United Kingdom*, Judgment of 25 April 1978, Series A no 26, at para 31: 'The Court must also recall that the Convention is a living instrument which, as the Commission rightly stressed, must be interpreted in the light of present-day conditions. In the case now before it the Court cannot but be influenced by the developments and commonly accepted standards in the penal policy of the member States of the Council of Europe in this field'.

[25] *Matthews v United Kingdom* (1999), para 39 (emphasis added).

[26] *Young, James and Webster v United Kingdom*, Judgment of 13 August 1981, Series A no 44.

with freedom of association under art 11 ECHR. The applicants in this case were rail workers in British Rail who had refused to enter a closed-shop agreement on the grounds that they disagreed with the political aims of the specified trade unions and who were later dismissed fairly under English law. Their argument in Strasbourg was that art 11 ECHR embodies a negative freedom of association, ie a right not to join a trade union—if one does not want to—without any negative consequences and that therefore dismissal for failing to be a member of a specified trade union amounts to a violation.

The UK Government argued that art 11 ECHR does not confer any right not to be compelled to join an association because this right 'had been deliberately excluded from the Convention', adding in proof the following passage in the preparatory works: [27]

On account of the difficulties raised by the 'closed-shop system' in certain countries, the Conference in this connection considered that it was undesirable to introduce into the Convention a rule under which 'no one may be compelled to belong to an association' which features in [Article 20 par. 2 of] the United Nations Universal Declaration.

It is clear in this passage that the drafters explicitly intended not to confer this right. Yet interestingly, the European Court did not find this decisive. Here is what it said:

Assuming for the sake of argument that, for the reasons given in the above-cited passage from the travaux préparatoires, a general rule such as that in Article 20 par. 2 of the Universal Declaration of Human Rights was deliberately omitted from, and so cannot be regarded as itself enshrined in, the Convention, it does not follow that the negative aspect of a person's freedom of association falls completely outside the ambit of Article 11 (art 11) and that each and every compulsion to join a particular trade union is compatible with the intention of that provision. To construe Article 11 (art 11) as permitting every kind of compulsion in the field of trade union membership would strike at the very substance of the freedom it is designed to guarantee.[28]

It then went on to find a violation of art 11 ECHR on the grounds that there was an illegitimate interference with the substance of the applicants' right to freedom of association.[29] Did the Court simply ignore the drafters' intentions? Three dissenting judges complained as follows:

Reference to the 'substance' of freedom of association is not relevant in the present context. Although the Court has often relied on the notion of the substance of the rights guaranteed by the Convention, it has done so only when the question was what

---

[27] *Young, James and Webster*, para 51.

[28] ibid para 52.

[29] The Court was, as always, careful to find a violation in the particular case, not regarding closed shops in general, and to note that compulsion to join a particular trade union may not always be contrary to the Convention. See *Young, James and Webster*, at para 55.

regulation or limitation of a right was justified. It has held that even in cases where regulation or limitations were allowed explicitly or by necessary implication, they could not go so far as to affect the very substance of the right concerned. In the present case, however, the problem is whether the negative aspect of the freedom of association is part of the substance of the right guaranteed by Article 11 (art 11). For the reasons stated above the State Parties to the Convention must be considered to have agreed not to include the negative aspect, and no canon of interpretation can be adduced in support of extending the scope of the Article (art 11) to a matter which deliberately has been left out and reserved for regulation according to national law and traditions of each State Party to the Convention.[30]

Both the government and the dissenting judges put great emphasis on the fact that the matter had been deliberately left out by the drafters, as a *decisive* factor against the finding of a violation. The Court however insisted that it is the *substance* of the right that is important, downplaying any significance drafting history may have.

Of course on occasion the European Court has employed originalist arguments. In *Bankovic*,[31] the Court, sitting as a Grand Chamber, had to decide whether NATO's bombing campaign in the former Yugoslavia fell within the jurisdiction of Contracting States under art 1 ECHR. In an unfamiliar fashion, and instead of sticking to its preferred method of 'evolutive interpretation', the Court rushed into invoking arts 31–32 of the VCLT, including the relevance of preparatory works.[32] The Court never explained in *Bankovic* why, unlike *Golder*, the object and purpose of the ECHR does not settle the question of jurisdiction so that there is need to resort to supplementary means of interpretation. Agreeing with the respondent governments' submissions (which had been prepared by the United Kingdom) the European Court endorsed an argument which it had repeatedly and expressly rejected since *Golder*: 'Had the drafters of the Convention wished to ensure jurisdiction as extensive as that advocated by the applicants, they could have adopted a text the same as or similar to the contemporaneous Articles 1 of the four Geneva Conventions of 1949'.[33] This is not to say of course that this reasoning was decisive in the Court's ruling the application inadmissible, or that the case was wrongly decided for that reason. But the idea that had the drafters wished to grant a right they could have adopted a different text, had certainly not counted against the applicant in *Golder*. Having said that, it is important to

---

[30] *Young, James and Webster*, Dissenting Opinion of Judge Sørensen, joined by Judges Thór Vilhjálmsson and Lagergren, at para 4.

[31] *Bankovic v Belgium and Others*, Admissibility Decision of 12 December 2001.

[32] ibid paras 17–21, 65, and 75. Note in particular the intentionalist character of the Court's argument in para 74.

[33] ibid para 75.

note that the Court in *Bankovic* used intentionalist arguments to interpret a non-substantive provision of the Convention (art 1 ECHR), ie a provision not dealing with the human rights but with general issues of public international law. It could well be that intentionalist or conventionalist methods of interpretation is justified for such provisions.

The Failures of Originalism

Is the European Court's rejection of originalism justified? It sounds counter-intuitive to suggest that neither the text nor drafters' intentions are relevant in solving interpreting difficulties and for good reason. One needs to be careful not to oversimplify the critique against originalism. It is the particular way in which either the text or drafters' intentions are taken into account under originalist theories that raises concerns. This section aims to show that originalism cannot be the correct theory of interpretation by default but that it is in need of some normative foundation, just like non-originalist theories.

Let us first examine more carefully the idea that judges must show fidelity to the text. Many people are inclined to believe that creative interpretation in law is always objectionable because it goes beyond 'the text'. Faced with someone who insists his novel interpretation is covered by the text, they usually complain: 'if this were the case then the text would mean whatever each one wants it to mean'. Yet, we do not think this is a self-evident argument in other forms of interpretation. We do not think, for instance, that we must interpret food recipes strictly, or else: 'they will mean whatever each one wants them to mean'. On the contrary, we usually take it for granted that we can interpret recipes in a way that matches our tastes. Textualism is therefore an unfortunate name for a theory of adjudication if it purports to ground its normative claims on the mere fact that there is a text there to interpret. There are no general theories of textual interpretation. Different theories of interpretation may be applicable to texts of law, literature, food recipes, medical prescriptions, sports playbooks, practical jokes, school regulations, etc.

But more importantly, textualism is an unfortunate label to the extent that it advocates strict interpretation in order to avoid recourse to extra-textual arguments. For surely it is itself an extra-textual theory: very rarely, if ever, does the text of the law itself stipulate that interpretation must be strict rather than creative. It is nowhere written in the ECHR that the European Court should interpret the Convention in a strict way. Textualism is not grounded within the 'four corners' of the document, so to speak. And even if it was, this would not necessarily be the end of the argument.

Yet we would be unfair to textualism if we were to neglect a fact that makes originalist theories possible. This fact is, I believe, indisputable: it is that the circumstances of human life change constantly and along with them, change our beliefs regarding how to understand important things about ourselves and the world we live in. What was yesterday's pride often becomes today's shame and what was yesterday's crazy claim often becomes today's widely shared paradigm. Equality is a famous example. People used to believe (including the drafters of the US Constitution) that segregation does not violate equality. We, on the other hand, now take race discrimination as a paradigm case of not treating people as equals. Moreover, we often take changes in belief to constitute substantive discoveries, rather than a mere change in our preferences. We feel we make progress in many areas of human knowledge: we do not simply say that equality prohibits race discrimination because that is how we like to think of equality now.

Changes in beliefs inevitably affect the meaning we feel inclined to attribute to concepts. To be sure, evolution in beliefs takes place slowly and in a piecemeal fashion. Some people might defend old meanings against new beliefs; others might feel strongly that the new meaning has always been part of the concept. Disagreement, not just in law but everywhere, is always located within this background of evolution and constant reinterpretation. Originalism insists that the interpretation of the law be insulated from evolution and that substantive disagreement does not contaminate judicial practice. It insists that, in the light of substantive disagreement amongst citizens over fundamental concepts of political morality, judges should not be the ones to decide which interpretation offers the best understanding as a matter of law. In other words, originalism is a theory that defends, not the text or drafters' intentions as such, but an interpretive option in need of some further normative justification.

It is also important to note that the idea of respecting drafters' intentions does not, by itself, call for any particular style of interpretation, be it strict, purposive, evolutive, or other. Consider the idea that the interpretation of the law must not change over time but must always remain faithful to the intentions of the drafters. We can first imagine cases where the drafters themselves expressly authorized courts to revise or update the interpretation of the text. Suppose it is enacted (either in a constitution or in an international human rights treaty) that:

Inhuman and degrading treatment is prohibited. A treatment is inhuman or degrading only if it is supported by the best moral arguments available to the court at each given time and regardless of drafters' or the community's views on the matter.

Clearly, a judge applying this provision would have to attribute different meaning depending on the views of the community at each given time. Hence what was not prohibited as inhuman and degrading in the 18th century may be prohibited now and vice versa. It would be the judge's duty, out of respect for the drafters, to adjust the meaning of the provision to contemporary circumstances. Were he or she to attribute a fixed meaning he or she would be disregarding their will.

The example purports to make the point that drafters' intentions come in different kinds and at various levels of abstraction. Take the ECHR. Drafters in 1950 had an *abstract* intention to promote and safeguard human rights in Europe but they also had a more *concrete* intention about which situations, in their view, human rights cover.[34] To be sure, the ECHR would never have existed if some officials in the Contracting States had not intended to draft, sign, and make it legally binding. Which is however more crucial: their intention to protect a list of fundamental freedoms of their citizens, whatever these may be (intentions of principle), or their intention to protect what they, 50 years ago, believed these freedoms to be (intentions of detail)?

Presumably, drafters had the former intention as much as they had the latter: they had a concrete idea of what human rights there are but it was their more abstract belief in the moral objectivity and universality of these rights that led them to draft the ECHR following the Second World War atrocities. Objectivity, however, denotes a certain kind of mind-independence: like any of us, drafters may have been wrong about morality's demands. Which intention did drafters take as more dominant? Their concrete intention to be bound by what they thought these moral rights were, or their more abstract intention of being bound by whatever moral standards the human rights in the Convention really enact?

One may be tempted to suggest that we should try to discover which of the two (and perhaps at which level) were thought to be more important by the drafters themselves. This is to introduce a third kind of intention, what is called the drafters' meta-intentions.[35] It is possible that the drafters felt more strongly about their abstract intention to protect the fundamental moral rights that people are indeed entitled to rather than their concrete intention to protect those rights that they, 50 years ago, believed individuals are morally entitled to.[36] Recall that in his dissent in *Golder*, Judge Fitzmaurice welcomed the possibility that the convention makers could expressly authorize the Court to

---

[34] The distinction between abstract and concrete intentions is taken from Dworkin. See Dworkin R, 'The Forum of Principle' in *A Matter of Principle* (1985) at ch 2; Dworkin R, *Life's Dominion* (1993) at ch 5 and Dworkin R, 'Comment' in Gutman A, *A Matter of Interpretation* (1997) at 115.

[35] Also called 'interpretive' intentions, see Dworkin R, *A Matter of Principle* (1985) at 52.

[36] Dworkin argues that in the case of the American constitution we might invoke various facts in support of this claim: that the rights are framed in abstract rather concrete wording and that the drafters could not have thought their views were the final ones in moral matters.

expand, through interpretation, the scope of the Convention rights. He just required that their meta-intentions be clearly expressed.

It is worth noting that the distinction between abstract and specific intentions is not foreign to international law. Consider the long-standing controversy about the remedy that should follow the determination of an invalid reservation. Various options are available. First, the state may not be bound by the provision as to which the reservation was made, but continue to be bound by the rest of the treaty. Secondly, the state may cease to be a party to the treaty altogether and be no longer bound by it. Thirdly, the reservation may be severed and the state may remain bound the entire treaty, including the provision as to which the reservation was made. Ryan Goodman has proposed to solve this controversy by looking at relevant evidence of what was the ratifying state's intent: would the state have ratified the convention if they knew that their reservation could be severed? Was, in other words, the reservation an essential condition for ratifying the treaty? [37]

Yet introducing all these kinds of intentions involves a clear issue of circularity. For we begin by distinguishing between the various intentions that states (or drafters) have: concrete, abstract, and meta-intentions. We then take their meta-intentions as being the most important ones, which in turn direct us to either their concrete or their abstract intentions. Here is the circularity: we ask what is the way in which drafters' intentions become relevant, and we answer this question by saying that they become relevant in the way in which drafters intended. Even if states (or drafters) had meta-intentions (which they may not always do), we can only defer to them on the basis of some other reason, not on that of intentions. Suppose that a state's meta-intention directs us to its concrete rather than abstract intention. Why, one may ask, is its meta-intention more important than its abstract intention?[38] At this point, intentionalism runs out of justificatory resources. The question is not whether states' (or drafters') intentions are relevant but *which* of their intentions are relevant in interpretation.

In conclusion, any theory of interpretation for the ECHR (or any international treaty) must at some stage stand outside drafters' intentions and

---

[37] See Goodman R, 'Human Rights Treaties, Invalid Reservations and State Consent' 96 *American Journal of International Law* (2002) 531. This is precisely the application of the idea that, since states had both concrete (not to be bound by a specific provision) and abstract intentions (to enter the treaty), we should be looking at their meta-intentions, at what they thought was their dominant intention. Not surprisingly, Goodman's argument is that this method has the advantage of maintaining respect for state consent as opposed to taking severance of reservations as a compromise to state consent.

[38] Cf Dworkin's point in *A Matter of Principle* (1985) at 53, talking about drafters' meta-intention: 'Why is it not our view against theirs on a complex issue of political theory, so that if our reasons are good we should not abandon these reasons just because people in another age would have disagreed?'

provide a normative justification based on values of political morality. Dworkin notes this very well in the context of constitutional interpretation:

Some part of any constitutional theory must be independent of the intentions or beliefs or indeed acts of the people the theory designates as Framers. Some part must stand on its own in political or moral theory; otherwise the theory would be wholly circular.[39]

This idea captures, I believe, the spirit of arts 31–32 VCLT. We cannot know whether (and the extent to which) drafters' intentions are relevant unless we settle first on the object and purpose of the treaty. How to read drafters' original intentions is the result of, rather than an alternative to, a theory about the object and purpose of the treaty.

The Object and Purpose of the ECHR

It is not hard to see that part of what motivates originalist theories is fear of judicial creativity coupled with ideas of democratic legitimacy. In the face of controversy over the application of a constitutional provision, it is better to defer to the views of those who had the right to legislate in the first place than to leave the matter to be decided by a handful of unelected judges. The originalist could say something analogous about international law and the principles of state consent and equality of sovereign states: in the face of controversy over the application of a treaty, it is better to defer to state consent which is a valid source of state obligation than to allow individual judges to impose new obligations upon sovereign states. Indeed this was precisely what Sir Gerald Fitzmaurice advocated in *Golder*.

Yet there are a number of difficulties with these arguments. Often the drafters of a constitution were wholly unrepresentative of the people in the first place (as in the case of the fathers of the American constitution) or have become unrepresentative of the people as it stands now, say because of a change in its territorial boundaries through war or unification with a neighbouring state. Why should their views be taken into account given that they lack or lost a democratic basis? Similarly in the case of international treaties, the original Drafting States may now have become a minority of Member States.[40] Why should the drafting history be taken into account and not, say, the understanding of the new Member States—now forming a majority— either at the time of joining or even their current one?

---

[39] Dworkin R, *A Matter of Principle* (1985) at 54.

[40] As it actually has in the case of the ECHR: there are now 46 Member States compared to the 10 founding states of the Council of Europe (Belgium, Denmark, France, Ireland, Italy, Luxembourg, the Netherlands, Norway, Sweden, and the United Kingdom).

But perhaps the most serious difficulty with the above views is the implicit assumption that ideas of democratic legitimacy or state sovereignty are *sufficient* to justify any legal provision. To put it rather extremely: a legal provision, be it in a constitution or an international treaty, instituting slavery would not have any legally binding force even if it were passed by a democratically chosen constitutional convention, or even if all states expressly agreed to it. Dramatic as it may be, the example shows that ideas of democratic legitimacy at domestic level or state consent at international level cannot be the only values when considering how and which legal obligations are created. This is particularly so in the case of human rights. We do not think that the question whether torture or genocide is permissible is governed by the principle of state consent. Why should we think that state consent is important when interpreting an international human rights treaty?

So even if drafters' concrete intentions or meta-intentions are closer to the notion of state consent, the originalist is wrong to assume that this notion underpins human rights treaties. The nature of fundamental human rights is such that they provide the conditions under which state consent should be respected and states (or parliaments) can legitimately pursue their goals. Hence the originalist argument that evolutive interpretation of human rights might offend state consent is simply irrelevant. It is the nature of human rights treaties, and the kind of value they serve that directs us to look at drafters' more abstract intentions and ignore their concrete or meta-intentions.

Is there any other value that the originalist can invoke in support of certainty or strict interpretation of human rights treaties? It is often argued in domestic law that *publicity* is a distinctive virtue that law should have.[41] It is a good thing to have laws that are promulgated officially and are publicly available for everybody to read. This is because people form expectations in their lives and they must be able to know in advance what it is that they are bound by in order to arrange their behaviour accordingly. It is generally thought wrong to hold people accountable for violating standards they could not possibly know they were bound by. On this view, the idea of protecting people's expectations calls for both certainty and stability in the interpretation of the law.

I have serious doubts as to whether law is an instrument for protecting people's expectations or people's welfare in general. But even if that were true, the application of this idea to international law would still appear problematic as it is hard to see why surprising Contracting States is morally wrong.[42] What kind of harm does a state suffer when its expectations regarding its treaty obligations are defeated? It is difficult to think of states as agents who

---

[41] See Fuller L, *The Morality of Law* (1964) at 34–35, 43–44.

[42] Recall that the argument that states must know exactly what they get themselves into, so to speak, by joining the ECHR was made by Fitzmaurice in his separate opinion in *Golder*.

form expectations about their lives so that it becomes morally problematic to surprise them. In domestic law we assign weight to expectations because of the importance they have for the autonomy of the person affected. It is thought that defeating their expectations is problematic because of the value of *personhood* or *agency*:[43] individuals live a for a relatively short time during which they set higher ends and plans of life to pursue at the expense of day-to-day satisfaction of lower desires. This type of autonomy cannot in any sense be attributed to states whose legal personality and continuity is not reducible to that of natural persons.[44]

True, dynamic interpretation of human rights might surprise Contracting States in that they often have to introduce legislative measures in order to comply with their Convention obligations. These measures may be quite extensive, involving, among other things, financial costs that will affect the community as a whole. That is why states very often make interpretive declarations to treaties to ensure that certain provisions will be interpreted in the way that state expects them to be interpreted. But again, it is difficult to argue that we must balance this inconvenience suffered by states against the human rights that an individual is entitled to under the ECHR. If the Court is convinced that the applicant is entitled to a remedy as a matter of human rights should the fact that his state will be inconvenienced count against him? The moral force of human rights is precisely that they should not enter into cost-benefit calculations. To have a right is to be entitled to be treated in a certain a way even if the community would be better off by violating it. The purpose of human rights treaties, unlike that of many other international treaties, is to protect the autonomy of individuals against the majoritarian will of their state, rather than give effect to that will.

In sum, the values of the ECHR, its object and purpose, fully justify why the Convention must not be interpreted in terms of what the drafters thought in 1950, or to put it accurately, why it should not be interpreted in terms of the drafters' *concrete* intentions back in 1950.

Evolutive Interpretation: Truth Not Current Consensus

It may be suggested that evolutive interpretation amounts to a rejection of drafters' intentions and original meaning but does not sever the links with how Member States understand the Convention rights. Perhaps the Court revises its standards of interpretation according to what the *current* consensus

---

[43] On the connection between this value and human rights see Griffin J, 'First Steps in an Account of Human Rights' 9 *European Journal of Philosophy* (2001) 306.

[44] On the relation between state and personal autonomy see Beitz C, *Political Theory and International Relations* (1999, with afterword) at 71–83.

within Contracting States is. This suggestion smacks of moral relativism as it suggests that the Court interprets the Convention in order to apply present-day conventional standards regardless of their content. But is it true? Looking at the relevant case law, it seems to me that the Court introduced the notion of the ECHR as a living instrument with a view to understand better the principles that underpin the rights of the Convention, regardless of how states themselves apply these principles.

The method of evolutive interpretation first appeared in *Tyrer,*[45] where the Court had to decide whether judicial corporal punishment of juveniles amounts to degrading punishment within the meaning of art 3 of the Convention. The punishment, having the form of bare-skin birching carried out by a policeman at a police station, was prescribed by law and practiced in the Isle of Man, a dependent territory of the United Kingdom with a significant degree of legislative autonomy. At that time, judicial corporal punishment had been abolished in the rest of the United Kingdom and was neither to be found in the vast majority of the other Contracting States. In his submissions, the Attorney General for the Isle of Man put forward an interesting argument: judicial corporal punishment could not be considered degrading because it 'did not outrage public opinion in the Isle of Man'.[46]

The Court took issue with this communitarian conception of degradation, ie the view that degrading is whatever public opinion and the community at large thinks is degrading. In its ruling, the Court noted that public acceptance of judicial corporal punishment could not constitute a criterion as to whether it is degrading or not, because the reason why people favour this type of punishment may well be the fact that corporal punishment is degrading and can therefore operate as a deterrent. The Court, in other words, rejected the view that communal reactions provide some privileged insight to the truth of the protected right. A few lines earlier, the Court had noted that in assessing whether a particular punishment is degrading one must look at all the circumstances of the case and 'in particular the *nature* and context of the punishment itself and manner and method of its execution'.[47] There is a stark contrast here between what public opinion thinks about birching and what is the real character of this punishment.

The Court then went on to relate its reasoning with a different category of common beliefs. It said:

The Court must also recall that the Convention is a living instrument which, as the Commission rightly stressed, must be interpreted in the light of present-day conditions. In the case now before it the Court cannot but be influenced by the developments and

---

[45] *Tyrer v United Kingdom*, Judgment of 25 April 1978, Series A no 26.
[46] ibid para 31.
[47] ibid para 30 (emphasis added).

commonly accepted standards in the penal policy of the member States of the Council of Europe in this field.[48]

This piece of legal reasoning inaugurated the Court's extensive use of evolutive interpretation. It puts the emphasis upon present-day conditions as an important factor in interpreting the Convention and attaches great importance to the common standards that are found in the legislation of the Member States of the Council of Europe, rather than anywhere else.

Surprisingly however, the Court never made clear how the notion of a 'living instrument', applied in the case at issue, led to a specific decision. There was no reference to Member States' criminal law, no comparative study done on judicial corporate punishment and no attempt to establish that the abolition of corporal punishment is a commonly accepted standard in the Council of Europe. Even if we assume that the Court took this to be common knowledge, we find no explicit link in the judgment between what is commonly accepted regarding corporal punishment and the Court's reasoning in reaching its decision. The Court made use of what is commonly accepted in any apparent way. Having elegantly pronounced the 'living instrument' approach, the Court went on to base its decision on purely substantive considerations. It said that 'the very *nature* of judicial corporal punishment is that it involves one human being inflicting physical violence on another human'[49] and that it is an institutionalized assault on a person's dignity and physical integrity, which is precisely what art 3 of the Convention aims to protect. It further added that the institutionalized character of the punishment, the fact that it is inflicted by total strangers to the offender and the fact that it is administered over the bare posterior, all add up to the punishment being degrading. The Court accordingly found a violation of art 3 of the Convention.

In *Marckx*,[50] decided just a few months after *Tyrer*, the applicants, a child born out of wedlock and his unmarried mother, complained—among others—that Belgian legislation violated their right to family life under art 8 of the Convention, and discriminated against them contrary to art 14 of the Convention. Belgian law at the time did not confer maternal affiliation by birth alone with respect to 'illegitimate children', contrary to the so-called *mater certa sempre est* maxim. Unlike the case of 'legitimate children', maternal affiliation between a child born out of wedlock and its mother could only be established either by voluntary recognition or by a court declaration.

The Court noted straightforwardly that art 8 makes no distinction between 'legitimate' and 'illegitimate' family and that such distinction would anyway contradict art 14 of the Convention, which prohibits any discrimination

---

[48] ibid para 31.
[49] ibid para 33 (emphasis added).
[50] *Marckx v Belgium*, Judgment of 13 June 1979, Series A no 31.

grounded on birth.[51] It then noted that 'respect for family life' may well impose positive obligations on the part of the state and further argued that Belgian law puts illegitimate family under unfavourable and discriminatory conditions.[52] At that point the Court was faced with an objection raised by the Belgian government. The respondent government conceded that the law favoured the traditional family but maintained that 'this was in the purpose of ensuring the family's full development as a matter of objective and reasonable grounds relating to morals and public order'.[53] The Court took issue at the Belgian government's objection. While admitting that at the time when the Convention was drafted it was regarded permissible to distinguish between 'legitimate' and 'illegitimate' families, it emphasized that 'the domestic law of the great majority of the Member States of the Council of Europe has evolved and is continuing to evolve, in company with the relevant international instruments, towards full juridical recognition of the maxim *mater semper certa est*.[54]

There is an important difference between *Tyrer* and *Marckx*. In the latter the Court went on to refer explicitly to two international conventions (the Brussels Convention on the Establishment of Maternal Affiliation of Natural Children and the European Convention on the Legal Status of Children Born out of Wedlock) as a way to demonstrate the existence of 'commonly accepted standards'. In doing so, the Court moved away from construing commonly accepted standards as solely those found in the legislation of Member States as these two international conventions were far from being signed by the majority of the Contracting States at the time. But the Court noted that, 'the existence of these two treaties denotes that there is a clear measure of common ground in this area amongst *modern societies*'. It added further that Belgian law itself shows signs of this 'evolution of rules and *attitudes*'.

This shift from commonly accepted standards in domestic legislations to signs of evolution of attitudes amongst modern societies is particularly noteworthy. Commonly accepted standards found in legislation were not a necessary component of what counts as present-day conditions. The Court was satisfied to show and to emphasize that the distinction between 'legitimate' and 'illegitimate' families was no longer regarded appropriate in European societies. Whether or not this attitude is reflected in the majority of domestic legislation was not so decisive. In *Marckx*, 'living instrument' meant, above all, keeping pace with evolving European attitudes and beliefs, rather than with some specific legislation to be found in the majority of Member States.

The introduction of this abstract standard of common European attitudes and beliefs manifests how loose the requirement of consensus became in

---

[51] ibid para 31.
[52] ibid paras 36–39.
[53] ibid para 40.
[54] ibid para 41.

Marckx. For there is an apparent difficulty in construing this 'common ground among modern societies'. Does it mean what all or most citizens accept? Or does it rather mean what reasonable and fully informed citizens would accept? Moreover, how is the Court to say when this common ground has been achieved? By consulting opinion polls? By relying on judges' limited personal experience? To be sure, none of these worries arose in *Marckx*. The Court did not explain how this common ground among societies is to be found. On the contrary, such assertion was a mere addition to a chain of substantive reasoning: the Court had said, independently, that the distinction between 'legitimate' and 'illegitimate' children is discrimination based on birth, that 'illegitimate' children were left motherless for a period of time and that illegitimate families faced unfavourable circumstances in law. The Court did not say that modern societies no longer accepted the distinction between 'legitimate' and illegitimate families, therefore there was a violation of the right to family. Rather, the Court argued that the above distinction violates the right to life as a matter of what this right really amounts to and that *in addition*, this is becoming common ground in modern societies.

In a series of later judgments, the Court proceeded in the exact same way: it examined the legal issue involved thoroughly, made claims and assumptions about the purpose of the protected right and explained in detail why governmental acts fall short of serving this purpose.[55] Nowhere did it subscribe to a conventionalist approach to interpretation: it is not the case that what constitutes a violation changes whenever rules and attitudes change. Its reasoning clearly implied the idea of a substantive *discovery*: the complaint behaviour has always constituted a violation, even when it was not considered to be so.

In the well-documented *Dudgeon* the main issue was whether penalization of homosexuality in Northern Ireland violated the right to respect for family life guaranteed by art 8 para 1. The Court held that:

As compared with the era when that legislation was enacted, there is now a better understanding, and in consequence an increased tolerance, of homosexual behaviour to the extent that in the great majority of the member States of the Council of Europe it is no longer considered to be necessary or appropriate to treat homosexual practices of the

---

[55] In *Guzzardi v Italy*, Judgment of 6 November 1980, Series A no 39, for example, the Court had to decide whether compulsory residence on an island constitutes deprivation of liberty. The Italian Government argued that all that the applicant had suffered was not a deprivation but a restriction of liberty, which is outside the scope of art 5. In response the Court held that 'the difference between deprivation and restriction is one of degree or intensity and not one of nature or substance', that deprivation may take several forms and that 'account must be taken of a whole range of criteria such as the type, duration, effects and manner of implementation of the measure in question'. It concluded that the applicant's condition amounted to deprivation of liberty even though there was no physical barrier to the applicant's movement. Towards the end of its judgment the Court made reference to 'the notions currently prevailing in democratic states'. Again, it is difficult to see how the Court's substantive account was in any sense 'a prevailing notion'.

kind now in question as in themselves a matter to which the sanctions of the criminal law should be applied.[56]

It then went on to find a violation of the respective right. Although there is an apparent effort in the quoted passage to base its reasoning on what is now believed in the great majority of the Member States, it is equally striking that the Court takes contemporary understanding in Member States to be *better* and not merely different than the time when anti-homosexual legislation was enacted. So it is not enough to there being a different understanding evolved, this understanding must also be better, ie towards the truth of the substantive protected right.

The above case law shows that the Court was primarily interested in evolution towards the moral truth of the ECHR rights, not in evolution towards some commonly accepted standard, regardless of its content. First, the Court does not take the time to look at domestic legislations in some comparative exercise and aggregate what most states do. Secondly, its reasoning is informed by substantive considerations about the protected right, not by a common denominator approach. Third, it emphasizes that evolution is important in that it results in a better understanding of the ECHR rights.

In sum, the Court applied a first-order moral reading of the ECHR rights, adding hesitant and redundant remarks about this being somehow commonly accepted. The above case law suggests that: (a) there is an objective substance or value of the protected right; (b) evolution is important only because and so far as it gets this value right; and (c) for the evolution to constitute a standard of correctness for the ECHR, it is not necessary to establish a concrete consensus among the majority of Contracting States. The idea is more that of a hypothetical consensus: given the principles we now believe underlie the Convention, how would reasonable people agree to apply these principles to concrete human rights cases?

A careful reading of the 'living instrument' approach reveals that it is nothing more than a reiteration of the Court's principle in autonomous concepts cases: the protected rights are not 'theoretical or illusory but practical and effective' and should not be subordinated to states' 'sovereign will'. The ECHR rights give effect to important moral principles. If these moral principles are independent of what most states thought back in the 1950s then they are also independent of what most states think now. [57]

---

[56] *Dudgeon v United Kingdom*, Judgment of 22 October 1981, Series A no 45, at para 60.

[57] Cf *Law's Empire*, at 368: 'Some clauses, on any eligible interpretation, recognise individual rights against the state and nation: to freedom of speech, to due process in criminal procedures, to treatment as an equal in the disposition of public resources, including education. Stability in the interpretation of each of these rights taken one by one is of some practical importance. But since these are matters of principle substance is more important than that kind of stability'. On the question whether we should treat bills of rights as transparent or opaque statements, see also Brink D, 'Legal Theory, Legal Interpretation and Judicial Review' 17 *Philosophy and Public Affairs* (1988) 105.

4

Two Concepts of the Margin
of Appreciation

[W]hen the Court has in its hands an abundance of elements leading to
the conclusion that the test of necessity is satisfied by itself and embarks
on a painstaking analysis of them, reference to the margin of appreciation should be duly confined to a subsidiary role.[1]

Judge Christos Rozakis

Introduction

What is the 'margin of appreciation' that states are afforded regarding their
human rights obligations under the European Convention on Human Rights
(ECHR)? Most commentators complain about the lack of a uniform or coherent application of the margin of appreciation doctrine in the case law of the
European Court of Human Rights.[2] The controversy is reinforced by the fact
that the doctrine is not found in the text of the Convention but was developed
by Strasbourg organs themselves. The two main monographs on the margin
of appreciation provide an exhaustive list of all the cases where the European
Court of Human Rights has used the doctrine, the first chronologically[3] and
the second by Convention article.[4]

I propose to analyse the margin of appreciation doctrine, as it figures in the
case law, in a different way by drawing a distinction between two different ways
in which it has been used by the Court. The first one, which I shall call the *substantive* concept of the doctrine, is to address the relationship between individual

---

[1] Judge Christos Rozakis, Dissenting Opinion in *Odiévre v France* (2004) 38 EHRR 43.
[2] See Macdonald R, 'The Margin of Appreciation' in Macdonald, Matscher, and Petzold (eds)
The European System for the Protection of Human Rights (1993) 85.
[3] Yourow H, *The Margin of Appreciation Doctrine* in the Dynamics of European Human Rights
Jurisprudence (1996).
[4] Arai-Takahashi Y, *The Margin of Appreciation Doctrine and the Principle of Proportionality in
the Jurisprudence of the ECHR* (2002).

freedoms and collective goals. The second one, which I shall call the *structural* concept, is to address the limits or intensity of the review of the European Court of Human Rights in view of its status as an international tribunal. It amounts to the claim that the European Court should often *defer* to the judgment of national authorities on the basis that the ECHR is an *international* convention, not a national bill of rights. The ideas of subsidiarity and state consensus are usually invoked to support the structural use of the margin of appreciation.

It is my view that much of the confusion and controversy surrounding the margin of appreciation is due to the Court's failure to distinguish between these two ideas in its case law. The Court uses the same term (margin of appreciation) both for saying that the applicant did not, as a matter of human rights, have the right he or she claimed, and for saying that it will not substantively review the decision of national authorities as to whether there has been a violation. This explains why the doctrine is described as 'the other side of the principle of proportionality' by some[5] and as enabling 'the Court to balance the sovereignty of Contracting Parties with their obligations under the Convention' by others.[6] I hope that if the two concepts are distinguished on the basis of the possible values each one serves, this will enable the European Court to impose some coherence and transparency on its reasoning and avoid charges of inconsistency and arbitrariness. But I do not mean to endorse the distinction between these two different uses as a normatively important one. In fact, under a certain understanding of the moral character of human rights and of the role of judicial review, the use of the doctrine is altogether unjustified.

Theories of International Human Rights Law

The distinction I wish to draw within the European Court's case law, between the substantive and the structural concept of the doctrine, is not the distinction between having an ideal moral theory of resolving conflicts between rights and public interest on one hand, and having to defer to the decisions made by some authority on the other. For whether or not a court should defer to the decisions of another body (eg the legislature or the executive, or the domestic judiciary) depends on which set of principles we assign to the bill of rights at issue. It is those principles, ie the normative content attributed to the treaty as a whole, that will tell us whether and how decisions of another body carry interpretive weight. Rather, the distinction is between cases where no violation is found because the Court believes that the applicant's human rights have not been violated, and cases where the Court will not declare a

---

[5] ibid at 14.
[6] Macdonald R, 'The Margin of Appreciation' in Macdonald, Matscher, and Petzold (eds) *The European System for the Protection of Human Rights* (1993) 123.

violation or will not fully scrutinize decisions made by national authorities for reasons having to do with the status of the ECHR as an international convention. It is the *reason* for which the Court reaches the conclusion that there was no violation that characterizes both uses of the concept.

Should all the reasons for or against ruling a violation of the ECHR turn on an account of human rights as a moral ideal? This need not be the case. We know that the content of the legal rights embodied in the ECHR is informed by the *morality* of human rights and the idea that we have certain moral rights by virtue of being human. The Convention protects certain universal human rights, not some *sui generis*, internationally agreed upon rights. It is clearly stated in the preamble that the Convention aims at 'securing the universal and effective recognition and observance' of certain rights declared by the Universal Declaration of Human Rights. Yet we also know that asserting a *legal* right is tantamount to making a claim about the content of past *political* decisions and the conditions under which these decisions justify the use of state coercion.[7] Although international law lacks a supranational coercive mechanism, propositions about the ECHR (and international human rights claims more generally) can be seen as claims about the obligations states have by virtue of being members of international organizations, such as the United Nations and the Council of Europe and parties to particular Conventions.[8] Recall that a Contracting State that breaches the ECHR has a duty under international law to abide by the final judgment of the Court (art 46 ECHR) and to award just compensation to the victim (art 41 ECHR). The Committee of Ministers of the Council of Europe is the political organ that supervises the execution of judgments. Under art 8 of the Statute of the Council of Europe, the Committee of Ministers may expel Contracting States that seriously violate their obligation to accept the principles of the rule of law and human rights and to collaborate sincerely in the realization of the aims of the Council.

The ruling of a violation of the ECHR is thus a mixture of two kinds of claims: a claim about the moral rights that individuals are entitled to by virtue of being human and a claim about the nature of obligations that states have undertaken by joining the ECHR. These two claims need not be identical. The power of the European Court to hold Contracting States accountable under the ECHR may not give full effect to the rights that individuals have by virtue of being human.[9]

---

[7] Cf. Dworkin R, *Law's Empire*, pp 93ff.

[8] As I argued in Chapter 1, one need not take justification of *state coercion* as a conceptually necessary feature of the point of all legal practices. For interpretive theories of law, the questions of whether legal practice has value, and if so, what that value is, are open. For discussion on whether Dworkin is committed to attributing this point to law and for related criticism see Dickson J, 'Methodology in Jurisprudence: A Critical Survey' 10 *Legal Theory* (2004) 117, at 141ff.

[9] Cf Griffin J, 'Discrepancies Between the Best Philosophical Account of Human Rights and the International Law of Human Rights' 10 *Telos* (2001) 133.

To put it in a slightly different way: the ECHR, as a legal document, shapes the moral principles upon which the Convention rights are founded. This may be so for various reasons and it is important to note a few. To begin with, there are human rights that are not protected by the ECHR (such as various economic and social rights) but are protected by other international conventions, like the International Covenant on Economic, Social and Cultural Rights (ICESCR) or the European Social Charter. Moreover, the Convention may explicitly restrict the scope of a human right, the extent of the right, and ways in which the right is legally protected. For instance, contrary to other human rights documents such as the ICCPR, the ECHR did not, until recently,[10] have a general non-discrimination clause. Protection against discrimination was limited to the rights recognized in the Convention. Finally, there may be moral theories of human rights that, though compatible with the text of the Convention, are ruled out or need to be qualified in the light of procedural aspects of the Convention, such as those governing the admissibility criteria. For example, under the new Protocol 14, an application will be inadmissible if the applicant has not suffered a 'significant disadvantage'.[11]

Still, any reason for or against ruling a violation must follow from a *principled* account of the point and purpose of the ECHR. And this account may include reasons that turn on the fact that the ECHR is an international convention in the context of a specific regional organization, ie the Council of Europe. A theory of interpretation of the ECHR will thus have to take into account and build on both the substantive moral ideas that underpin human rights and the textual and institutional particularities of the ECHR. The question, in other words, that we (and the European Court) should in the first place be asking when interpreting the Convention is not 'have this person's human rights been violated?' but rather, 'did the state breach its international law duties under the ECHR?' The aim, as a matter of law, is to find a coherent set of principles that we can plausibly attribute to the ECHR. It follows that we cannot have a theory of the ECHR that offends the moral values of human rights. Nor can we have a theory of international human rights that takes no account of the fact that the ECHR differs in nature from other international human rights treaties and from national bills of rights.[12] The ECtHR is under a judicial duty to justify its decisions and explain the real basis of

---

[10] Protocol 12 to the Convention for the Protection of Human Rights and Fundamental Freedoms which contains a general prohibition of discrimination entered into force on 1 April 2005.

[11] On Protocol 14 see Greer S, 'Protocol 14 and the Future of the European Court of Human Rights' *Public Law* (Spring 2005) 83–106.

[12] Cf the discussion in ch 1. Comparisons between what different human rights courts have decided on specific rights are too quick: there is no reason to assume in advance that national constitutional courts, regional supranational courts, and global human rights committees should reach the same result in interpreting specific rights. The decisions of these different bodies are

its judgments. Adjudication must be principled and Courts must provide transparent principles of interpretation.

In what follows I shall present and contrast the two uses of the margin of appreciation, as found in the case law of the European Court, with a view to identify principles that can justify them. In relation to the substantive concept of the margin of appreciation, the Court seems to interpret it as the tension between individual freedoms and collective goals. I shall argue that this tension can be accommodated by many moral theories of human rights and that neither the text of the Convention nor the case law are decisive on which moral theory underlies the ECHR. Whether or not interference with individual freedoms is justified by and large turns on the much broader issue of the role of human rights as a matter of political morality, rather than the concepts of the margin of appreciation or deference. What counts as legitimate interference with these rights as a matter of political morality is discussed in the next chapter.

The Court's use of the structural concept, on the other hand, is based on the idea that national authorities are better placed to decide certain human rights cases, most notably in cases where there is no consensus among Contracting States in matter of public morals. I survey the relevant case law and highlight the principles that can be used to justify it. The final section concludes by exploring the possible connections between the two uses of the doctrine and by raising some doubts about the doctrine altogether.

The Substantive Concept of the Margin of Appreciation

The substantive concept of the margin of appreciation addresses the relation between fundamental freedoms and collective goals, under an ideal theory of political morality. In the Court's case law, the margin of appreciation is usually linked to the following two propositions: first, that state authorities are justified[13] in taking measures, prescribed by law, in order to advance collective goals; and secondly, that although such measures may interfere with fundamental freedoms of the individual, such interference may not amount to a violation of his or her rights.[14]

---

primarily propositions of the law of the respective instrument, not accounts of the concept of a particular human right.

[13] It is an important issue whether and when states may sometimes be *under an obligation* to take such measures, in the sense of a positive duty to interfere with someone's right for the sake of protecting rights of others. In *Handyside v United Kingdom* (1979–80) 1 EHRR 737, the ECtHR observed that restrictions under the accommodation clauses are of an optional character.

[14] I prefer this formulation to the distinction between a prima facie interference with a right and an 'all things considered' violation (or non-violation). I wish to avoid the suggestion that rights (as opposed to fundamental freedoms) can be interfered with to a lesser or greater extent.

The second of these propositions is particularly crucial regarding the margin of appreciation. The substantive concept of the doctrine refers to all the cases where despite the fact that there was 'interference' with a freedom protected by the ECHR, the interference did not amount to a violation of a right. As such, it presupposes or is linked to a theory which tells us whether and when interference with fundamental freedoms is impermissible.

The substantive concept of the margin of appreciation is most clearly exhibited in the so-called 'accommodation' or 'limitation' clauses found in arts 8–11 of the ECHR and other international human rights documents, like the ICCPR.[15] It is there provided that state authorities may interfere with the exercise of a right in pursuit of legitimate aims such as national security, public safety, economic well-being, prevention of crime, etc.[16] In other words, it is not the case that there is an absolute legal prohibition against 'interfering' with the Convention freedoms. The same moreover can be said about Convention articles that do not have accommodation clauses but allow for exceptions (eg right to life under art 2 ECHR) or limit the application of the right to particular circumstances (right to liberty and security and right to fair trial under arts 5 and 6 ECHR). For example, the fact that individuals have a right to life does not mean that deprivation of life by state officials is never justified under the Convention.

The margin of appreciation has paradigmatically figured in judgments concerning the accommodation clauses in arts 8–11 ECHR. The link between the margin of appreciation and the fact that fundamental freedoms admit of restrictions under the accommodation clauses has been part of Strasbourg's case law from its very early years. In the 'Vagrancy' judgment in 1971, the court said:

> [T]he competent Belgian authorities did not transgress in the present cases the limits of the power of appreciation which Article 8(2) of the Convention leaves to the Contracting states: even in cases of persons detained for vagrancy, it was 'necessary' to impose restrictions for the purpose of the prevention of disorder or crime, and the protection of the rights and freedoms of others.[17]

The accommodation clauses leave states a 'power' or 'margin' of appreciation to interfere with those Convention freedoms. Such interference may however be found to be impermissible, if the conditions set out in the second paragraph of arts 8–11 ECHR are met. In interpreting this paragraph, Strasbourg

---

[15] See eg arts 18 para 3, 19 para 3, 20, and 22 para 2 of the ICCPR. The margin of appreciation has however also been used in ECHR articles that have no accommodation clause. For a full list of the articles in which the doctrine has been used see Arai-Takahashi Y, *The Margin of Appreciation Doctrine and the Principle of Proportionality in the Jurisprudence of the ECHR* (2002).

[16] See arts 8 para 2, 9 para 2, 10 para 2, 11 para 2, and Protocol 1 art 1 para 2 ECHR.

[17] *De Wilde, Ooms and Versyp v Belgium* ('Vagrancy case') (1979–80) 1 EHRR 373, para 93.

organs apply the following four-stage test: they examine, first, whether there was an interference with a Convention freedom; then, whether the interference was prescribed by law; thirdly, whether the purpose of the interference falls within the list of legitimate aims mentioned in the accommodation clauses; and, finally, whether the interference was proportionate or 'necessary' in a democratic society or whether there was a 'pressing social need' for it.

The principle of proportionality is by far the most important and most demanding criterion for whether the limitation of a right was permissible under the Convention. If the interference is found to be proportionate or 'necessary in a democratic society', then the Convention right has not been violated. This explains why some commentators directly link the principle of proportionality to the margin of appreciation. Arai-Takahashi for example calls the principle of proportionality 'the other side of the margin of appreciation'[18] and Matscher characterizes it as 'corrective and restrictive of the margin of appreciation'.[19]

I take this 'limitability' or non-absoluteness of the Convention freedoms to be the main idea behind the substantive concept of the margin of appreciation. This idea is sometimes related to the view, very familiar within modern liberal democracies, that there must be a fair balance between individual rights and collective goals. The Court has endorsed this view:

> The Court agrees with the Commission that some compromise between the requirements for defending democratic society and individual rights is inherent in the system of the Convention. ... As the Preamble to the Convention states, 'Fundamental Freedoms ... are best maintained on the one hand by an effective political democracy and on the other by a common understanding and observance of the Human Rights upon which (the Contracting States) depend'.[20]

The Court reads the accommodation clauses as an invitation to decide whether a 'fair balance' was struck between individual freedoms and collective goals in a particular case. This being the case, however, it follows that for the purposes of both examining whether interference is permissible and expressing the outcome of this examination, reference to the margin of appreciation is superfluous. The idea of the margin of appreciation in itself clearly lacks any normative force that can help us strike a balance between individual rights and public interest. Whether the complained acts fall within or outside the margin of appreciation, whether, that is, the interference with the freedom is

---

[18] Arai-Takahashi Y, *The Margin of Appreciation Doctrine and the Principle of Proportionality in the Jurisprudence of the ECHR* (2002) at 14.

[19] Matscher F, 'Methods of Interpretation of the Convention' in Macdonald, Matscher, and Petzold (eds) *The European System for the Protection of Human Rights* (1993) 79.

[20] *Klass v Germany* (1979–1980) 2 EHRR 214.

permissible all things considered, is what the Court in each case is asking. It cannot answer this question on the basis that the complained acts fall within the state's margin of appreciation. This would beg the question.

Many commentators have noted this very well. Macdonald for example writes: 'If the Court gives as its reason for not interfering simply that the decision is within the margin of appreciation of national authorities, it is really providing no reason at all but is merely expressing its conclusion not to intervene, leaving observers to guess the real reasons which it failed to articulate'. [21] And Rabinder Singh notes: 'The margin of appreciation is a conclusory label which only serves to obscure the true basis on which a reviewing court decides whether or not intervention in a particular case is justifiable. As such it tends to preclude courts from articulating the justification for and limits of their role as guardians of human rights in a democracy'.[22]

These commentators rightly complain as Strasbourg often uses the margin of appreciation to express a *final* conclusion as to whether a *particular* interference with an individual right amounts to a violation *all things considered*, ie once the proportionality test has been applied. This is, for instance, the case when it is decided that some national authority, which is justified in pursuing a legitimate aim prescribed by law, *overstepped* its margin of appreciation and violated a right. Here is an example:

In the light of these various factors, the Court reaches the conclusion that no fair balance was struck between the interests of the private health insurance company on the one side and the interests of the individual on the other. In these circumstances, the Court considers that the German authorities overstepped the margin of appreciation afforded to them under paragraph 2 of Article 8.[23]

And vice versa, Strasbourg organs often conclude that the authority in question did not violate a right, as it acted *within* its margin of appreciation. Here is another example:

The Court further finds that, in the particular circumstances of the instant case, the resultant interference was proportionate to the legitimate aim pursued. In this connection, it is noteworthy that the applicant's sentence was substantially reduced on appeal and, most significantly, his prison sentence was quashed by the Sieradz Regional Court. In sum, it cannot be said that the national authorities overstepped the margin of appreciation available to them in assessing the necessity of the contested measure.[24]

---

[21] See Macdonald, 'The Margin of Appreciation', at 85.
[22] Singh R et al, 'Is there a role for the "Margin of Appreciation" in national law after the Human Rights Act?' 1 *European Human Rights Law Review* (1999) 4.
[23] *Van Kuck v Germany* (2003) 37 EHRR 973 at paras 84–85.
[24] *Janowski v Poland* (2000) 29 EHRR 705 at para 35.

In these and other cases, the idea of the margin of appreciation is not used to express a general point about the limitability of rights but to express a final determination as to whether the state has violated a right in some particular case. I noted earlier that in cases where no other theory, such as the principle of proportionality, has been used to reach this final determination, the Court has simply failed to provide reasons for its decision. But using the term 'margin of appreciation' to express a final determination on a particular case is still problematic even when proportionality has called all the shots. It conveys the misleading image that the logical space occupied by an authority's margin of appreciation is tantamount to all the acts (or omissions) that that authority may undertake without violating any rights. This, however, is putting the cart before the horse. We have no prior theory of what falls within the states' margin of appreciation which we can use to find out what state acts (or omissions) amount to a violation. Rather, we use other tools, such as 'balancing' or the proportionality principle in order to find out the limits of the Convention rights.

One of the ECtHR judges has eloquently captured this in a recent concurring opinion:

I am fully in agreement with the conclusion reached by the majority of the Grand Chamber that there has been no violation of Article 8 of the Convention in this case. Yet I would like to express a different point of view with regard to the reasoning which led to that conclusion, and more particularly with regard to the weight that the majority attaches to the margin of appreciation enjoyed by the French State in the circumstances of the case.

I do not deny of course that, in the absence of common European standards on matters of child abandonment in conditions of secrecy and anonymity, France enjoys a certain margin of appreciation in determining the modalities of divulging information on the identity of the parties; and the Court correctly refers to it. Yet, it seems to me that, in its reasoning, the Court has overstressed this particular aspect of the margin of appreciation to the detriment of showing that it has struck a proper and satisfactory balance between the limited margin of appreciation enjoyed by France and the test of necessity (necessary in a democratic society), which for me is the crucial test to be applied in the circumstances of the case. Indeed, when, as in the present case, the Court has in its hands an abundance of elements leading to the conclusion that the test of necessity is satisfied by itself and embarks on a painstaking analysis of them, reference to the margin of appreciation should be duly confined to a subsidiary role.

If one reads the judgment carefully, one realises that the Court has proceeded to an analysis of the competing interests involved, applying explicitly or implicitly its own case law in order to find which of the competing interests of the applicant, on the one hand, and of democratic society on the other are more worthy of protection and for which reasons.[25]

---

[25] *Odièvre v France* (2003), concurring opinion of Judge Rozakis.

Judge Rozakis is here complaining that the Court's reasoning was driven by a substantive analysis of the competing interests involved (ie the applicant's or those of a democratic society) and that the final judgment as to whether there was a violation or not turned on whose interests were more worthy of protection and for which reasons. The idea of the margin of appreciation neither figures nor is required in that reasoning.

In sum, where the Court has used what I call the substantive concept of the doctrine, it was to make a very general and simple point about the limitability or non-absoluteness of the Convention rights. It does not and cannot settle the question of whether a particular interference with a Convention right is permissible. References to the doctrine in particular judgments are either superfluous or question begging.[26]

Still, we are left with an important question: when is an interference with a Convention right proportionate? What is the correct theory to apply in order to strike the correct 'balance' between individual rights and collective goals? Does the idea of the 'permissible interference' square with the moral force of human rights?

The accommodation clauses in arts 8–11 ECHR provide that in order to be permissible, the interference must be 'necessary in a democratic society' and give a list of legitimate aims, which varies from article to article. But these clauses leave open a number of questions as to how the test of proportionality should be construed. Should the interference be deemed necessary, if it is merely rationally connected to and advances one of the legitimate aims? Or should it also be the case that there is no other alternative, which advances the goal equally well but does not interfere, or interferes less with, the right in question? If so, who must bear the burden of proof as to the existence of a less restrictive alternative? Should we, further, take into account the weight and the character of the pursued aim itself? And are there, finally, cases where the interference is the least intrusive possible in order to advance a legitimate aim, yet it still amounts to a violation because it infringes the 'core' of the right in question?

I noted earlier that the limitability of rights is usually related to the idea that there is an inherent tension between individual freedoms and collective goals. We should expect that both this idea and the method that the Court uses to resolve this tension presuppose a particular theory of human rights as moral rights. Yet the balancing between the various conflicting interests often

---

[26] Needless to say, one could argue that the Court should stop using the term margin of appreciation whenever the issue is to do with the moral basis of human rights, as opposed to the limits of judicial review of the European Court, by virtue of the fact that the ECHR is an international convention (structural margin of appreciation). I choose to refer to claims about the moral basis of rights as the *substantive* concept of the margin of appreciation only because the Court keeps using the label when it applies the proportionality test, often without offering a basis for its final conclusion.

takes place ad hoc in the absence of a normative theory. This has naturally appeared arbitrary, particularly in view of the general requirement that courts must justify their decisions. The substantive margin of appreciation must refer to a theory that explains the role of rights within a broader scheme of political morality that includes political values such as justice, legality, and democracy. Without locating rights within such a scheme we would be unable to provide a useful and illuminating account of such notions as proportionality and deference. I take up this task in the next chapter.

The Structural Concept of the Margin of Appreciation

Many commentators view the margin of appreciation as a feature of a supranational judicial system, designed to balance the sovereignty of the contracting states with the need to secure protection of the rights embodied in the Convention.[27] On the structural concept, the margin of appreciation imposes limits on the powers of judicial review by virtue of the fact that the ECHR is an international convention. It is the idea that the Court's power to review decisions taken by domestic authorities should be more limited than the powers of a national constitutional court or other national bodies that monitor or review compliance with an entrenched bill of rights.

Under the structural concept of the doctrine, state authorities enjoy a margin of appreciation, in that the Court will not substantively scrutinize their decision. Their margin has to do with the relationship between the European Court of Human Rights and national authorities, rather than with the relationship between human rights and public interest. Eva Brems notes that the margin of appreciation is the '"natural product" of the distribution of powers between the Convention institutions and the national authorities who share the responsibility for enforcement'.[28] It is used in cases to express the degree to which the Court will rely on an earlier decision of the national authorities and refrain from second-guessing whether, in its own view, the right has been violated. This is what commentators usually refer to as *deference*.

The main argument that supports the structural concept of the margin of appreciation seems to be an argument about the *institutional competence*, of the Court vis-à-vis that of national authorities. The ECtHR has argued in its case law that it must *defer* to the national authorities whenever they are *'better placed'* than an international judge to decide on human rights issues raised by

---

[27] See Helfer L and Slaughter AM, 'Toward a Theory of Effective Supranational Adjudication' 107 *Yale Law Journal* (1997) 273, at 316–17.

[28] Brems E, 'The Margin of Appreciation Doctrine in the Case-law of the European Court of Human Rights' 56 *Zeitschrift Für ausländisches öffentliches Recht und Völkerrecht* (1996) 240, at 304.

the applicant's complaint.[29] The argument from institutional competence is usually coupled with the principle of subsidiarity; the idea that the ECtHR is an international court whose task is to protect human rights on a *subsidiary* basis.[30]

There are two broad categories of cases in which the Court has taken national authorities to be better placed and has deferred to their judgment. The first category includes cases where there is no *consensus* among Contracting States on what human rights individuals have. The approach of the European Court has been that the less consensus there is among Contracting States on whether something counts as a human rights violation, the better placed national authorities are to decide on the matter, and the more deferential the European Court has to be in its review. This use of the margin of appreciation has, by and large, been used when interpreting personal sphere rights (arts 8–11 ECHR) and in particular restrictions based on public morals. The idea has been that in the absence of a uniform conception of public morals in Europe, Member States are 'better placed' to assess local values and their application to particular cases. This stance has been criticized as lending weight to the idea of moral relativism and compromising the universality of human rights.[31]

The second category comprises cases where the Court defers to the decision of the national authorities because the latter are better placed to decide on politically sensitive issues within a particular Contracting State. This category includes the case law on derogation under art 15 ECHR. The Court has been very reluctant to review whether derogation under art 15 ECHR is justified, on the basis that national authorities are 'better placed' to assess the exigencies of the situation. In *Ireland v United Kingdom*, the Court said:

It falls in the first place to each Contracting State, with responsibility for 'the life of the nation,' to determine whether that life is threatened by a 'public emergency', and, if so, how far it is necessary to go in attempting to overcome the emergency. By the reasons of their direct and continuous contact with the pressing need of the moment, the national authorities are in principle in a better position than the international judge to decide both on the presence of such as emergency and on the nature and scope of the derogations necessary to avert it. In this matter article 15 paragraph 1 leaves the authorities a wide margin of appreciation.[32]

---

[29] Although the Court usually adds that it will review the complained acts and that national supervision goes 'hand in hand with European supervision'. See *Handyside v UK*, para 49.

[30] See Ryssdall R, 'The Coming of Age of the European Convention of Human Rights' 18 *European Human Rights Law Review* (1996) 24.

[31] See Benvenisti E, 'Margin of Appreciation, Consensus and Universal Standards' 31 *New York University Journal of International Law and Politics* (1998–1999) 843.

[32] *Ireland v United Kingdom* (1979–80) 2 EHRR 25, para 207. See also *Brannigan and McBride v United Kingdom* (1994) 17 EHRR 539, para 43; *Aksoy v Turkey* (1997) 23 EHRR 553, para 68; and *Demir and Others v Turkey* (2001) 33 EHRR 43, para 43.

The Court's deferential stance in derogation cases has been heavily criticized by many commentators.[33] Other cases where the Court defers to the judgment of the national authorities, on the basis that they are better placed, include right to property cases,[34] town and planning policies,[35] and national courts' decisions on the best interest of the child.[36] A reason usually cited for relying on the judgment of national authorities in these cases, particularly in matters of fact, is the need to avoid *duplication of procedures* at the international level and the idea that the Court should not be turned into *a fourth instance* court. In the next section I shall discuss in more detail the case law on consensus, which by and large has been the main area in which the structural concept of the margin of appreciation has been used.

Consensus and Public Morals

Consensus as a basis for deference first appeared in the well-documented *Handyside v UK*.[37] The applicant in this case was the publisher of the 'Little Red Schoolbook', a book containing information on sexual matters for adolescents. The publication was seized and confiscated as obscene by the UK authorities and Handyside was sentenced to payment of a fine. The applicant complained that this amounted to a violation of his freedom of expression (art 10 ECHR). In its judgment, the Court first satisfied itself that the restrictions imposed on Handyside were both prescribed by law and in pursuit of a legitimate aim mentioned in the accommodation clause of art 10 para 2 ECHR, namely the protection of morals in the United Kingdom. It then went on to examine whether the restrictions imposed against the applicant in

---

[33] See Gross O and Aolain FN, 'From Discretion to Scrutiny: Revisiting the Application of the Margin of Appreciation Doctrine in the Context of Article 15 of the European Convention on Human Rights' 23 *Human Rights Quarterly* (2001) 625; Gross O, '"Once More unto the Breach": The Systemic Failure of Applying the European Convention on Human Rights to Entrenched Emergencies' 23 *The Yale Journal of International Law* (1998) 437; Marks S, 'Civil Liberties at the Margin: the UK Derogation and the European Court of Human Rights' 15 *Oxford Journal of Legal Studies* (1995) 69.

[34] *James v United Kingdom* (1986) 8 EHRR 123, para 46; *Lithgow v United Kingdom* (1986) 8 EHRR 329, para 122; *Former King of Greece v Greece* (2001) 33 EHRR 516, para 87; *Pincova and Pinc v Czech Republic*, Reports 2002-VIII, para 47; *Brannigan and McBride v United Kingdom*, para 43; *Gasus Dosier-und Fordertechnik GmbH v Netherlands* (1995) 20 EHRR 403, para 60; *Malama v Greece* (2001), Reports 2001-II, para 46; *Jokela v Finland* (2003) 37 EHRR 26, para 52; *Jahn v Germany* (Apps 46720/99, 72203/01, and 72552/01), Judgment of 22 January 2004, para 80.

[35] *Gillow v United Kingdom* (1986) 11 EHRR 355, para 56; *Buckley v United Kingdom* (1996), para 75.

[36] *Soderback v Sweden* (1998) 29 EHRR 95, para 33; *Buscemi v Italy*, Reports 1999-VI, para 55; *Hokkanen v Finland* (1994) 19 EHRR 139, para 64.

[37] *Handyside v United Kingdom* (1979–80) 1 EHRR 737.

order to protect public morals were 'necessary in a democratic society'. The Court said:

[I]t is not possible to find in the domestic law of the various Contracting States a uniform European conception of morals. The view taken by their respective laws of the requirements of morals varies from time to time and from place to place, especially in our era, which is characterised by a rapid and far-reaching evolution of opinions on the subject. By reason of their direct and continuous contact with the vital forces of their countries, State authorities are in principle in a better position than the international judge to give an opinion on the exact content of these requirements as well as on the 'necessity' of a 'restriction' or 'penalty' intended to meet them.…Consequently, Article 10 para. 2 leaves to the Contracting States a margin of appreciation. [38]

In *Sunday Times v UK*,[39] decided three years later, the Court had to rule on the prohibition on the publication of an article by *The Sunday Times*. The article referred to children who had been born with serious malformations of limbs because their mothers had used thalidomide during pregnancy. An English court had prohibited the publication to prevent 'contempt of court' as claims for damages were at the time pending before it. In its judgment, the European Court accepted that the prohibition served a legitimate aim, that of maintaining the authority and impartiality of the judiciary. While examining whether the restriction on freedom of expression was proportionate, the Court noted:

Again, the scope of the domestic power of appreciation is not identical as regards each of the aims listed in Article 10 (2) (art. 10-2). The Handyside case concerned the 'protection of morals'. The view taken by the Contracting States of the 'requirements of morals', observed the Court, 'varies from time to time and from place to place, especially in our era', and 'State authorities are in principle in a better position than the international judge to give an opinion on the exact content of these requirements'. Precisely the same cannot be said of the far more objective notion of the 'authority' of the judiciary. The domestic law and practice of the Contracting States reveal a fairly substantial measure of common ground in this area. This is reflected in a number of provisions of the Convention, including Article 6, which have no equivalent as far as 'morals' are concerned. Accordingly, here a more extensive European supervision corresponds to a less discretionary power of appreciation.[40]

It appears that the Court again relates the extent to which national authorities are 'better placed' to decide whether or not there is a 'fairly substantial measure of common ground' in the domestic law and practice of the Contracting States. The Court said clearly that, unlike the idea of morals, the idea of maintaining the authority of the judiciary finds a lot of common ground among

---

[38] ibid para 48.
[39] *The Sunday Times v United Kingdom* (1979–80) 2 EHRR 245.
[40] ibid para 59.

Contracting States, and is, *for that reason*, a 'far more objective notion'. Interestingly, contrary to *Handyside*, in *The Sunday Times* the Court found a violation.

The idea that national authorities are 'better placed' to decide on questions of morals because there is no uniform European conception, figures in a series of later judgments on freedom of expression. *Muller and Others v Switzerland* concerned the confiscation of obscene paintings at an exhibition and the conviction of the artist. The Court reiterated that 'today, as at the time of the *Handyside* judgment, it is not possible to find in the legal and social orders of the Contracting States a uniform European conception of morals'.[41] In *Otto-Preminger-Institut v Austria*, the Court had to examine whether the seizure and forfeiture of Werner Schroeter's film 'Liebeskonzil' (Council in Heaven) was a violation of the right of artistic expression. The film was thought by the Roman Catholic Church to be offending and the Austrian authorities instituted criminal proceedings on the grounds that the film 'disparaged religious doctrines'. The Court noted that the aim of the restriction was that of protecting the rights of others, which is legitimate under art 10 para 2. In particular the Court referred to the right 'not to be insulted in [one's] religious feelings by the public expression of views of other persons'.[42] In examining whether the restriction was proportionate to the aim pursued, the Court said:

> As in the case of 'morals' it is not possible to discern throughout Europe a uniform conception of the significance of religion in society . . . even within a single country such conceptions may vary. For that reason it is not possible to arrive at a comprehensive definition of what constitutes a permissible interference with the exercise of the right to freedom of expression where such expression is directed against the religious feelings of others. A certain margin of appreciation is therefore to be left to the national authorities in assessing the existence and extent of the necessity of such interference.[43]

In *Wingrove*[44] the applicant was a film director who had written and directed a video work entitled 'Visions of Ecstasy'. The video portrayed a woman dressed as a nun, and intended to represent St Teresa, having a sexual fantasy involving the crucified figure of Christ. The British Board of Film Classification rejected the applicant's application for a classification certificate, on the grounds that the video was obscene and contravened the British blasphemy law. In its judgment, the Court followed its previous case law in accepting the existence of a right not to be insulted in one's religious feelings by the public

---

[41] *Muller and Others v Switzerland* (1991) 13 EHRR 212, para 35.
[42] *Otto-Preminger-Institut v Austria* (1995) 19 EHRR 34, para 48.
[43] ibid para 50.
[44] *Wingrove v United Kingdom* (1997) 24 EHRR 1.

expression of views of other persons.[45] Protecting this right therefore constitutes, according to the Court, a legitimate aim under art 10 para 2 ECHR. In examining whether the interference with the applicant's freedom of expression was proportionate, the Court said:

A wider margin of appreciation is generally available to the Contracting States when regulating freedom of expression in relation to matters liable to offend intimate personal convictions within the sphere of morals or, especially, religion. Moreover, as in the field of morals, and perhaps to an even greater degree, there is no uniform European conception of the requirements of 'the protection of the rights of others' in relation to attacks on their religious convictions. What is likely to cause substantial offence to persons of a particular religious persuasion will vary significantly from time to time and from place to place, especially in an era characterised by an ever growing array of faiths and denominations. By reason of their direct and continuous contact with the vital forces of their countries, State authorities are in principle in a better position than the international judge to give an opinion on the exact content of these requirements with regard to the rights of others as well as on the 'necessity' of a 'restriction' intended to protect from such material those whose deepest feelings and convictions would be seriously offended.[46]

The above passage was repeated word for word in the more recent case *Murphy v Ireland* (2003).[47] The case concerned the prohibition by the Irish Independent Radio and Television Commission on the broadcasting of a television advertisement submitted by the Irish Faith Centre, a bible–based Christian ministry in Dublin. The Court accepted, once more, that such restrictions serve legitimate aims. It endorsed the Irish Government's point that the prohibition 'sought to ensure respect for the religious doctrines and beliefs of others so that the aims of the impugned provision were public order and safety together with the protection of the rights and freedoms of others'.[48] Interestingly, despite abundant references to the fact that the states' margin of appreciation is not unlimited but 'goes hand in hand with European supervision', in none of the above cases (*Handyside, Muller, Otto-Preminger-Institut, Wingrove, Murphy*) did the Court declare a violation.[49]

---

[45] ibid paras 45–48.
[46] ibid para 58.
[47] *Murphy v Ireland* (2004) 38 EHRR 212, at para 67. For a criticism of the Court's judgment in this case see Geddis A, 'You Can't Say "GOD" on the Radio: Freedom of Expression, Religious Advertising and the Broadcast Media After Murphy v Ireland', 2 *European Human Rights Law Review* (2004) 181.
[48] ibid paras 63–64.
[49] I do not mean to imply, of course, that these cases were wrongly decided just because the Court found no violation. I only wish to highlight that whenever the Court makes reference to the lack of consensus among Contracting States and to the idea that national authorities are better placed, its final judgment is usually against the applicant. I am therefore interested in assessing the merits of the structural concept of the margin of appreciation because it appears strongly to

The structural conception of the margin of appreciation was extended to other articles of the Convention. Strasbourg's case law on the rights of transsexuals is an excellent example of the idea that consensus among Contracting States should be a fundamental interpretative principle. The question there was not whether the applicant's right to private life had been proportionately restricted for the sake of a legitimate aim, but whether the state has a positive duty, under art 8 ECHR, to recognize officially the new gender identity of post-operation transsexuals and to alter public records accordingly. In *Rees v United Kingdom*,[50] the first major judgment on the issue, the Court stated that there was, at the time, little common ground among Contracting States in this area. When it revisited the same question, four years later, the Court was again interested in whether a consensus on the status of transsexuals had in the meantime emerged. It decided, however, that this was 'still, having regard to the existence of little common ground between the Contracting States, an area in which they enjoy a wide margin of appreciation'.[51] Eight years later, the Court was once more called to rule on the same matter in *Sheffield and Horsham v United Kingdom* (1998). The Court ruled that despite some legislative trends, it continued 'to be the case that transsexualism raises complex scientific, legal, moral and social issues, in respect of which there is no generally shared approach among the Contracting States'. [52]

Ruling in favour of the applicants was thus once more denied, albeit the Court's majority had begun to shift progressively from twelve votes to three in 1986 (*Rees*) to eleven votes to nine in 1998 (*Sheffield and Horsham*). Indeed, in 2002 the balance shifted radically and the Court in *Goodwin v United Kingdom* and *I v United Kingdom*[53] reversed its case law, ruling unanimously in favour of the applicants. In these two almost identical rulings, the Court first noted that it must have regard to 'the changing conditions within the respondent State and within Contracting States generally' and respond to any 'evolving convergence as to the standards to be achieved'.[54] In a section entitled 'the state of any European and international consensus' the Court argued that there were significant developments since its last ruling that justify departing from its previous case law.[55]

---

influence the Court's final determination. Needless to say, some of the above cases may have been correctly decided regardless of whether the Court was justified in using the structural concept of the margin of appreciation.

    [50] *Rees v United Kingdom* (1987) 9 EHRR 56, para 37.
    [51] *Cossey v United Kingdom* (1991) 13 EHRR 622, para 40.
    [52] *Sheffield and Horsham*, paras 57–58.
    [53] *I v United Kingdom* (2003) 40 EHRR 967.
    [54] *Goodwin v United Kingdom* (2002), para 74.
    [55] ibid paras 84–85. Interestingly, the Court noted that the lack of a common approach among the 46 Contracting States is hardly surprising and what is important is a 'clear and uncontested

Finally, in *Frette v France* the applicant complained that his application for authorization to adopt had been rejected on the basis of his homosexuality, and that this amounts to discrimination on the ground of sexual orientation, which is contrary to art 14 ECHR. The French Government submitted that the reason for the rejection was not the applicant's sexual orientation but the potential harm to the interests of the child to be adopted, if it is brought up by a homosexual and is deprived of a dual maternal and paternal role.[56] The applicant, on the other hand, argued that the prejudices of third parties against homosexual parenthood could not justify excluding him from adoption procedures because this would effectively amount to giving a right of veto to those motivated by such prejudices.[57] In its assessment, the Court found that the decision not to allow the applicant to adopt was indeed based decisively on his avowed homosexuality. It then went on to examine, as in all cases of alleged discrimination, whether the differential treatment complained of, was nevertheless based on an objective and reasonable justification. Having noted that consensus among Contracting States is of great relevance in this respect, the Court said:

It is indisputable that there is no common ground on the question. Although most of the Contracting States do not expressly prohibit homosexuals from adopting where single persons may adopt, it is not possible to find in the legal and social orders of the Contracting States uniform principles on these social issues on which opinions within a democratic society may reasonably differ widely. The Court considers it quite natural that the national authorities, whose duty it is in a democratic society also to consider, within the limits of their jurisdiction, the interests of society as a whole, should enjoy a wide margin of appreciation when they are asked to make rulings on such matters. . . . Since the delicate issues raised in the case, therefore, touch on areas where there is little common ground amongst the member States of the Council of Europe and, generally speaking, the law appears to be in a transitional stage, a wide margin of appreciation must be left to the authorities of each State.[58]

Having further mentioned that the interests of the children to be adopted are of paramount importance and that the scientific community is divided over the possible consequences of being adopted by one or more homosexual parents, the Court concluded that 'if account is taken of the broad margin of appreciation to be left to States in this area and the need to protect children's

---

evidence of a continuing international trend in favour not only of increased social acceptance of transsexuals but of legal recognition of the new sexual identity of post-operative transsexuals'. Cf also the more recent *Van Kuck v Germany* (2003) 37 EHRR 973, where the Court found a violation of art 6 and art 8 ECHR.

[56] *Frette v France* (2004) 38 EHRR 438, para 36.

[57] ibid para 35. The applicant cited the US Supreme Court decision, *Palmore v Sidoti* 466 US 429 (1984). [58] ibid para 41.

best interests to achieve the desired balance, the refusal to authorise adoption did not infringe the principle of proportionality'.

One wonders whether the Court would have reached a different decision if most European states allowed homosexuals to adopt, despite the uncertainty of the relevant scientific studies. Besides, the applicant's claim seems to have been that one of the main causes of potential psychological problems of children adopted by homosexuals is the very existence of social prejudice against homosexual parenthood. If this is the case, then prohibition against homosexuals adopting only reinforces this social prejudice and ruins permanently their chances of raising children free from psychological problems.

5

Liberal Principles of Human Rights Interpretation

If some men get their kicks by watching movies of women with big breasts engaged in fellatio, and if others get theirs by watching depictions of gang rape or flogging or mutilation, this really should not give rise to a claim on anyone's part not to be surrounded by, or even included in, such fantasies. We have no right to be free from the fantasies of others, however much we may dislike them.

Thomas Nagel[1]

Introduction

Are rights absolute? How are we to understand the limitations on rights in arts 8–11 ECHR? In the previous chapter I drew a distinction between the substantive and the structural concept of the margin of appreciation. The former is used by the Court to express a final conclusion on whether an interference with a Convention right is justified. I argued that this very important question turns on moral issues in the philosophy of rights which the Court often mutes but which it must inevitably address if it is to avoid charges of arbitrariness and inconsistency. In this chapter I examine the moral foundations of rights as found in the work of Anglo-American liberals with a view to draw insights about the principles that should govern the interpretation of the limitation clauses.[2]

Rights, Interests, and Reasons

It is widely held that there is an inherent tension between human rights and public interest and that there must somehow be a reconciliation or compromise

---

[1] Nagel T, 'Personal Rights and Public Space' 24(2) *Philosophy and Public Affairs* (1995) 83, at 106.

[2] I should stress that I do not intend to provide a theory of the moral foundations of all the rights found in the ECHR (such as prohibition from retrospective punishment, freedom from torture, right to fair trial, or right to property). My focus is on rights which have limitation clauses and in the interpretation of which the Court has used the notion of the margin of appreciation.

between the two.[3] This view makes particular sense within political theories that treat both rights and collective goals as protecting interests. It can be said that the rights and liberties listed in the ECHR protect some (perhaps the most fundamental) of the interests that individuals have.

Under simple forms of utilitarian theories, conflicts between individual and public interests do not pose a problem. In its simplest form, utilitarianism holds that acts are right or wrong simply by virtue of the goodness of their consequences (consequentialism), that the goodness should be measured in terms of people's preference or desire satisfaction (welfarism) and that we should always try to maximize utility (aggregation).[4] Interests protected by rights are entered into the utilitarian calculation on a par with other interests that individuals have; they are protected only if doing so produces the maximum amount of preference satisfaction. For example, according to a crude version of utilitarianism, we have a duty to punish an innocent person if the consequences of doing so will maximize utility, say by satisfying the majority's sense of security. Unsurprisingly, utilitarianism has been traditionally understood as the biggest enemy of rights which are commonly championed as an objection to it.

Tension between rights and collective goals only make sense within either anti-utilitarian moral theories (such as deontology or perfectionism) or some modified form of utilitarianism that aims at accommodating rights (such as rule-utilitarianism).

A rule-utilitarian model of rights would assign to the ECHR freedoms a form of *relative* priority:[5] they are to be protected unless they conflict with a very large quantity of (non-rights based) aggregated preferences. This model seems to fit the wording of the ECHR accommodation clauses and the legitimate aims in the interests of which rights may be restricted. For some of these aims, like the protection of morals or the economic well-being of the country, do not refer, at least directly, to interests served by the human rights recognized in the ECHR but to aggregated individual preferences, like living in a community with a dominant communal morality (protection of morals), or living in a country with a higher aggregate level of welfare (economic well-being). The idea that 'a sufficient quantity of the more mundane interests', as Waldron puts it, may outweigh interests protected by human rights can be found in some ECtHR judgments. An

---

[3] McHarg A, 'Reconciling Human Rights and Public Interest: Conceptual Problems and Doctrinal Uncertainty in the Jurisprudence of the European Court of Human Rights' 62 *Modern Law Review* (1999) 671.

[4] Frey RG, 'Act-utilitarianism' in LaFollette H (ed) *The Blackwell Companion to Ethical Theory* (2000) at 165.

[5] See Waldron J (ed) *Theories of Rights* (1984) at 15. Waldron distinguishes a weak priority interest model and a lexical priority model.

individual's interest in artistic expression, for example, has been found to be outweighed by a sufficient quantity of people's preference to protect public morals.[6]

One common use of the proportionality principle seems compatible with the rule-utilitarian model of rights. This is the idea that collective goals may restrict individual rights, but only if it is absolutely necessary for the promotion of the collective goal. The European Court of Human Rights refers to it as 'the less restrictive alternative doctrine':[7]

States are required to minimise, as far as possible, the interference with these rights, by trying to find alternative solutions and by generally seeking to achieve their aims in the least onerous way as regards human rights.[8]

On this understanding of the test of proportionality, the interests protected by rights enjoy a weak priority in that the government must seek to find alternatives that promote a collective goal equally well but do not interfere with these rights, before it can limit them. But in the absence of such alternatives, governments will be free to limit rights in order to promote majoritarian preferences. Suppose for instance that the majority in one country holds very strong ethical views against pornography, to the extent that the very idea that pornography is available for private consumption, and not just being exposed to it in public places, outrages them. Suppose, in other words, that the preference the majority has in relation to its public morals can only be served by a total ban. It seems that the rule-utilitarian model would have to see this prohibition as proportionate.

We do better to look for an explanation of the limitation clauses in non-utilitarian theories. The different types of non-utilitarian theories of rights are, I think, best captured by the distinction Jeremy Waldron draws between immunities theories and reason-blocking theories of rights.[9] An immunities conception of rights is a theory that protects fundamental *interests* of the individual. A reason-blocking conception of rights is a theory that blocks political decisions based on certain types of impermissible considerations. Immunities conceptions of rights are interest-based theories. According to interest-based theories, rights protect individual interests that are important enough so as

---

[6] See eg *Wingrove v United Kingdom* (1997) 24 EHRR 1.

[7] See Arai-Takahashi Y, *The Margin of Appreciation Doctrine and the Principle of Proportionality in the Jurisptudence of the ECHR*, at 15.

[8] *Hatton v United Kingdom* (2001) 34 EHRR 1, para 97.

[9] See the exchange between Richard Pildes and Jeremy Waldron: Pildes R, 'Why Rights Are Not Trumps: Social Meanings, Expressive Harms, and Constitutionalism' 17 *Journal of Legal Studies* (June 1998) 725; Waldron J, 'Pildes on Dworkin's Theory of Rights' 29 *Journal of Legal Studies* (January 2000) 301; Pildes R, 'Dworkin's Two Conceptions of Rights' 29 *Journal of Legal Studies* (January 2000) 309.

to impose duties on others (and the state) to respect and advance them.[10] Raz defines rights as follows:

'X has a right' if and only if X can have rights, and, other things being equal, an aspect of X's well-being (his interest) is a sufficient reason for holding some other person(s) to be under a duty.[11]

Individual interests in life, autonomy, security, free speech, etc, are seen as generating rights and corresponding duties both negative (non-interference) and positive (assistance). An interest theory of human rights suggests that there is a list of vital interests which are universally shared by all individuals (by virtue of their humanity) and which must be protected to a significant degree before other interests are taken into account. The theory is marked by an element of maximization.

Reason-blocking theories on the other hand have a deontological and agent-relative[12] character. The emphasis is not on whether—and the extent to which—individual freedoms are limited or individual interests are harmed. Rather, the emphasis is on whether the *reasons* for restricting liberty or harming an interest are permissible. In Dworkin's famous metaphor, rights are 'trump cards' individuals have to block policies that are based on impermissible considerations. An example of an impermissible consideration is that which contains an *external* preference, ie a preference that someone should 'suffer disadvantage in the distribution of goods or opportunities on the ground that others think he should have less because of who he is or is not or that others care less for him than they do for other people'.[13] But restrictions of liberty (or harm to interests) that are not based on impermissible justifications do not amount to violations of rights.

Limitations of rights make perfect sense under interest-based theories. They are justified whenever a particular freedom falling under a protected human right does not serve an important individual interest or does not serve it significantly. As Raz puts it, for instance, freedom of speech is more important than freedom to eat green ice creams.[14] Perfectionist theories will also balance the protection of individual rights with the promotion of public goods. This is because occasionally restricting a freedom may be necessary for the promotion of certain goods (eg a tolerant society) that are public in the

---

[10] Interest theories of rights have been defended by David Lyons, Joseph Raz, and Neil MacCormick. See Waldron J (ed) *Theories of Rights* (1984) at 6.

[11] Raz J, *The Morality of Freedom* (1998) at 166.

[12] On agent-neutrality and agent-relativity see Sen A, 'Rights and Agency' 11 *Philosophy and Public Affairs* (1982) 3–39 and Nagel T, 'Personal Rights and Public Space' 24(2) *Philosophy and Public Affairs* (1995) 83.

[13] Dworkin R, 'Rights as Trumps', in Waldron (ed) *Theories of Rights*, at 161.

[14] Raz J, *The Morality of Freedom*, at 246.

sense that they will serve everybody's interests (eg everybody's autonomy).[15]
A limitation then would be proportionate under an interest-based model
either because the freedom that is restricted in a particular case is not conducive to the promotion of an important interest or because promotion of the
interest must be balanced against the promotion of other interests or public
goods.

Recall also that rights, on the interest theory, are grounded on aspects of
someone's well-being and provide a reason for holding others to be under a
duty. Duties, however, do not, on the interest theory, stand to a simple one-
to-one correlation with rights, as Waldron points out.[16] Someone's interest or
well-being may be served to a lesser or greater extent. What the impact of various governmental policies will be on the well-being of people, however, is difficult to assess in advance. The exercise of the rights and liberties recognized in
constitutions and treaties need not always serve a fundamental interest. And
vice versa: some important interests may not be commonly understood as an
exercise of a human right, for instance, the interest people have in sleep.[17] As a
result, balancing and trade-offs will be quite frequent under the interest-based
model. There are many important interests that people have and many ways
in which these interests can be served or harmed.

This proliferation of interests and conflicts of rights is quite common in
European human rights adjudication compared to constitutional adjudication in the United States. This is no surprise given the political and historical
differences between them. The European tradition has been more welfarist
and less protective of individual rights such as free speech than the American
tradition. One has the impression that European courts take themselves to
be partners with the government in devising policies that protect individuals'
interests as opposed to an institutional check on it. Indeed, the ECtHR often
stresses that the limitations must not restrict or reduce the right in such a
way or to such an extent that the very essence of the right is impaired.[18] The
substantive concept of the margin of appreciation may refer to the minimum
level of protection that is required for the *judicial* protection of these interests.
This is perhaps what the Court means when it says that 'it is no part of the
Court's function to substitute for the assessment of the national authorities

---

[15] Raz argues that some civil rights promote a certain public culture which in turn contributes
to the well-being of all individuals; see Raz J, *The Morality of Freedom*, ch 10. It would follow
that the extent to which protection of a specific right promotes public goods in each given case is
relevant for defining the limits of that right.

[16] Waldron J, *Liberal Rights* (1993) at 212.

[17] See the *Hatton* case, where this interest was taken to fall under the right to private life under
art 8 ECHR.

[18] See eg *Sheffield and Horsham v UK* (1999) 27 EHRR 163, para 66.

any other assessment of what might be the best policy in the field'.[19] Courts set a *minimum* threshold of protecting the ECHR rights, allowing states a 'margin of appreciation', ie allowing them to differ as to how they achieve this threshold as well as to the degree of protection given above it.[20]

Now contrast how the reason-blocking model of rights would account for the limitation clauses one finds in human rights treaties. Under reason-blocking models, it is not the case that people have a right to specific liberties (such as speech, religion, or assembly) that are important for their interests; rather, they have a right not to be deprived of a liberty or an opportunity on an inegalitarian basis, such as that their conception of the good life is *inferior*. Specific human rights are particularly important when the majority is likely to attack individual liberties motivated by hostile external preferences, ie preferences that deny to some human beings their equal status as autonomous persons. The reason-blocking model focuses in other words on a particular way in which political communities must treat their members as equals rather than on how well some individual interests are served. What courts do when examining whether an interference with a right is 'proportionate' is screening governmental policies to filter out impermissible reasons. When these reasons are not present, then the interference with a protected liberty is proportionate. But when governmental policies are based on these reasons, then rights are activated and block the enforcement of these policies.

Note two important aspects of the reason-blocking theory. First, as Waldron notes, 'trumping contrasts with balancing'.[21] Rights thus understood can never be 'balanced' against public goods, general utility, or other interests in the way the interest-based model suggests. A person's right not to be deprived of a liberty on the basis that his or her conception of the good life is inferior, is absolute. Secondly, the reason-blocking model is more minimalist and less burdensome for judges. Courts are not asked to establish what interests human rights should serve, in what ways and to what extent.

This reason-blocking theory can also find some ground in the ECtHR case law, although admittedly less than the interest-based model. It captures, I believe, the role that the non-discrimination clause plays under art 14 ECHR. The Court's approach has been that art 14 may be violated in conjunction with a substantive right of the Convention, without this latter right itself having been violated. It also captures the decisions to uphold the rights of

---

[19] *Ashingdane v United Kingdom* (1985) 7 EHRR 528. Also in *Buckley v United Kingdom* (1997) 23 EHRR 101, para 75: 'It is not for the Court to substitute its own view of what would be the best policy in the planning sphere or the most appropriate individual measure in planning cases'.

[20] For the idea of a 'minimum level of compatibility' see Carozza P, 'Uses and Misuses of Comparative Law in International Human Rights: Some Reflections on the Jurisprudence of the European Court of Human Rights' 73 *Notre Dame Law Review* (1998) 1217, at 1228.

[21] Waldron J, 'Pildes on Dworkin's Theory of Rights', at 303.

homosexuals or transsexuals against the moralistic preferences of the majority in *Dudgeon*[22] and *Goodwin*,[23] although this is not to say that these decisions cannot be accommodated under an interest-based theory.

I believe, however, that a reason-blocking theory of rights best captures not only the anti-utilitarian and anti-perfectionist character of rights but also the status of human rights as legal rights, ie as rights that operate as conditions for the legitimate use of coercive force.[24] They capture the intuition, which seems to me to be correct, that judicial protection of rights is not about increasing or maximizing the extent to which certain individual interests are served. This intuition is also found, I think, in the work of two of the most important liberal thinkers, namely John Rawls and Ronald Dworkin, which is discussed next.

Liberal Egalitarian Theories of Rights: Rawls and Dworkin

Rawls's Theory of Rights

In *A Theory of Justice* (1971), John Rawls employs the device of a hypothetical contract between members of a community that are to choose principles of justice from an original position, that is, behind a veil of ignorance.[25] Rawls argues that they would distinguish between basic liberties on one hand and distribution of income and wealth on the other, giving lexical priority to the former.[26] In *A Theory of Justice* Rawls's first principle of justice (the Liberty Principle), is formulated as follows:

Each person is to have an equal right to the most extensive total system of equal basic liberties compatible with a similar system of liberty for all.[27]

These basic liberties are: political liberty (the right to vote and hold public office), freedom of speech and assembly, liberty of conscience and freedom of thought, freedom and integrity of the person, right to hold personal property, and freedom from arbitrary arrest.[28] The liberty principle has *lexical* priority over the second principle[29] in that 'infringements of the basic equal liberties

---

[22] *Dudgeon v United Kingdom* (1982) 4 EHRR 149.
[23] *Goodwin v United Kingdom* (2002) 35 EHRR 447.
[24] See the discussion in ch 1.
[25] They are behind a veil of ignorance in that they do not know a list of things about themselves and their society, such as: their place in society, their class or social status, their fortune in the distribution of natural assets and abilities, their intelligence and strength, their conception of the good life, their aversion to risk or liability, and the particular economic and political circumstances of their own society. See Rawls J, *A Theory of Justice* (1999 revised edn) at 118.
[26] ibid at 53.
[27] ibid at 266.
[28] ibid at 53.
[29] The second principle (what Rawls calls the Difference Principle) reads as follows: 'Social and economic inequalities are to be arranged so that they are both (a) to the greatest benefit of the least

protected by the first principle cannot be justified, or compensated for, by greater social and economic advantages'. Basic liberties, as Rawls puts it, can only be restricted for the sake of liberty. Trade-offs between the basic liberties and the social and economic advantages are not allowed, let alone trade-offs between basic liberties and average utilitarianism.

Why are these liberties fundamental? The following passage from the *A Theory of Justice* is illuminating:

> I assume that the parties view themselves as free and equal persons who have fundamental aims and interests in the name of which they think it legitimate for them to make claims on one another concerning the design of the basic structure of society. The religious interest is a familiar historical example; the interest in the integrity of the person is another. In the original position the parties do not know what particular forms these interests take; but they do assume that they have such interests and that the basic liberties necessary for their protection are guaranteed by the first principle. Since they must secure these interests, they rank the first principle prior to the second. The case for the two principles can be strengthened by spelling out in more detail the notion of a free person. Very roughly the parties regard themselves as having a highest-order interest in how all their other interests, including their fundamental ones, are shaped and regulated by social institutions. They do not think of themselves as inevitably bound to, or as identical with, the pursuit of any particular complex of fundamental interests that they may have at each given time, although they want the right to advance such interests (provided they are admissible). Rather, free persons conceive of themselves as beings who can revise and alter their final ends and who give priority to preserving their liberty in these matters. Hence, they not only have final ends that they are in principle free to pursue or reject, but their original allegiance and continued devotion to these ends are to be formed and affirmed under conditions that are free.

Rawls's list of basic liberties and their priority are based on a certain conception of the self. Individuals are seen as free and equal agents who can rationally choose, revise, or alter their conception of the good life. They lead an autonomous life when they determine their own final ends. This idea is often described as the value of personal autonomy, ie 'the value of the free individual adoption of ideals of excellence and of plans of life based on them'.[30] Basic liberties are the ones that enable people to choose, pursue, and revise their conception of the good, free from the interference of others. So important and fundamental is the principle of autonomy thus understood, that free and rational agents would not risk losing it for the sake of greater economic and social advantages.

---

advantaged and (b) attached to offices and positions open to all under conditions of fair equality of opportunity', ibid at 266.

[30] Nino C, *The Ethics of Human Rights* (1991) at 132.

Other liberals too draw this link between human rights and the sovereignty to determine one's own ends.[31] Thomas Nagel writes:

The radical communitarian view that nothing in personal life is beyond the legitimate control of the community if its dominant values are at stake is the main contemporary threat to human rights. Often, of course, it is invoked in bad faith by ruling minorities claiming to speak on behalf of the community. But not always. Sometimes the values and even the majorities are real, and then the only defense against them is an appeal to the form of moral equality that accords each person a limited sovereignty over the core of his personal and expressive life. My contention has been that this sovereignty or inviolability is in itself, and not just for its consequences, the most distinctive value expressed by a morality of human rights.[32]

Interest theorists too recognize the link between rights and autonomy. Raz, for instance, maintains that rights to traditional civil liberties are explained by the general interest people have in being autonomous. He writes:

The capacity to be free, to decide freely the course of their own lives is what makes a person. Respecting people as people consists in giving due weight to their interest in having and exercising this capacity. On this view respect for people consists in respecting their interest to enjoy personal autonomy.[33]

But how does Rawls's first principle of justice explain limitations and conflicts of rights? The system of basic liberties must be equal and most extensive. It would follow that a limitation on my basic liberty is unjustified (proportionate, if you like) if others have more of that basic liberty than I do or if I can have more of that liberty without restricting the basic liberties of others. But how do we measure liberty?

This criticism was levelled against Rawls's theory of basic liberties by HLA Hart.[34] Hart noted that conflicts between liberties cannot be resolved on the basis that a certain resolution yields a 'greater' or 'stronger' system of liberty for 'these phrases suggest that no values other than liberty and the dimensions of it, like extent, size, or strength, are involved'.[35] Rather, a criterion of the value of different liberties, Hart argued, must be used to settle the conflict.[36] Rawls's idea of 'the most extensive system of equal basic liberties', however, does not provide such a criterion nor does his point that the conflict can be

[31] See Nagel T, 'Personal Rights and Public Space' 24(2) *Philosophy and Public Affairs* (1995) 83; Griffin J, 'First Steps in an Account of Human Rights', 9 *European Journal of Philosophy* (2001) 306.
[32] Nagel T, 'Personal Rights and Public Space' at 106.
[33] ibid at 190.
[34] See his 'Rawls on Liberty and its priority' in Hart HLA, *Essays in Jurisprudence and Philosophy* (1993) at 223.
[35] ibid at 233.
[36] Cf also Dworkin's criticism of the idea of liberty as a 'commodity' in *Taking Rights Seriously*, at ch 12.

resolved from the point of view of the representative equal citizen in the light of his rational interests.[37]

In response to these criticisms, Rawls revised the first principle in his later books *Political Liberalism* (1993) and *Justice as Fairness: A Restatement* (2001) as follows:

Each person has the same indefeasible claim to a fully adequate scheme of equal basic liberties, which scheme is compatible with the same scheme of liberties for all.[38]

Rawls clarified that the liberty principle is not aimed at maximizing liberty or some other quantifiable value and that reference to the most extensive system of equal basic liberties in *A Theory of Justice* was misleading. Rather, basic liberties and their priority are to guarantee the 'political and social conditions that are essential for the adequate development and full exercise of the two moral powers of free and equal persons'.[39] These two moral powers refer to the capacity individuals have for a sense of justice on one hand, and the capacity for a conception of good on the other. The criterion for the significance of a particular liberty or right as well as for the resolution of conflicts between basic liberties is the exercise of the two moral powers in two fundamental cases.[40] The first case has to do with the first moral power and the application of the principles of justice in a society. Political liberties and freedom of thought are basic because they ensure the opportunity for the free and informed application of the principles of justice and make possible the free use of public reason.

The second case, which is connected with the second moral power, concerns the exercise of citizens' power of practical reason in forming, revising, and rationally pursuing such a conception over a complete life. Liberty of conscience and freedom of association are basic because they ensure the opportunity for forming, revising, and pursuing a conception of a good life. Rawls adds that the remaining basic liberties—ie liberty and integrity (physical and psychological) of the person and the rights and liberties covered by the rule of law—can be seen as necessary for the exercise of the basic liberties in the two fundamental cases mentioned above.

The revised theory does provide a more clear and thorough account of why the particular rights and liberties found in constitutional documents are protected and not others, and how to go about resolving conflicts of rights. Rawls writes:

[. . .] a liberty is more or less significant depending on whether it is more or less essentially involved in, or is a more or less necessary institutional means to protect, the full and

---

[37] See Rawls J, *A Theory of Justice*, at 179. Hart notes that the representative citizens do not have enough knowledge of the content of their interests to use it as a criterion.

[38] Rawls J, *Justice as Fairness: A Restatement* (2001) at 42. This is a slightly different wording to the one in Rawls J, *Political Liberalism* (1993) at 291: 'Each person has an equal right to a fully adequate scheme of equal basic liberties compatible with a similar scheme of liberties for all.'

[39] *Justice as Fairness: A Restatement*, at 45.

[40] ibid at 112.

informed exercise of the moral powers in one (or both) of the two fundamental cases. The more significant liberties mark out the central range of application of a particular liberty; and in cases of conflict we look for a way to accommodate the more significant liberties within the central range of each.[41]

Rawls notes that certain kinds of speech (such as libel and defamation of private persons) should not be protected because they have no significance for the free use of public reason to judge and regulate the basic structure. Similarly, incitement to imminent and lawless use of force are 'too disruptive of democratic political procedures to be permitted by the rules of order of public discussion'. He is moreover clear that the first principle does not involve any kind of maximization. It would be absurd, he argues, to say that the exercise of the two moral powers can be maximized, say by maximizing the number of deliberate affirmations of a conception of the good.[42] This clearly rejects the idea, discussed earlier, that rights must be protected and promoted to the greatest extent possible before other interests are even taken into account.[43] Not only does Rawls distinguish between liberties that serve the two moral powers and those that do not,[44] he also opposes the idea that the exercise of the two moral powers in the two fundamental cases is something that requires maximization or distribution of resources.

Rawls's comments provide valuable insights into the nature of rights and their limits. Rawls does not start with the idea that certain liberties are fundamental and must be protected at all costs. The way the original position is framed and the use of the veil of ignorance produces a theory of rights that has already taken into account the values of equality and autonomy.[45] People are treated as equals when they are able to choose and pursue a conception of the good life free from the interference of others. Rights do not protect interests whose protection should be maximized. Rather, rights protect liberties relating to the exercise of the two moral powers. When restriction on a certain liberty does not affect the exercise of the two moral powers then no right has been violated even if that liberty may be classified as an instance of a protected interest (say, speech).

In relation to the ECHR, we can say that, on Rawls's revised theory, something may be said to be within the states' margin of appreciation either because it does not at all affect the two moral powers, or because the restriction

---

[41] ibid at 113.

[42] Rawls J, *Political Liberalism*, at 333.

[43] Although, of course, Rawls's views in the first edition of *A Theory of Justice* did encourage this view.

[44] Rawls uses the idea of the 'central range of application' of these liberties. It seems to me that this captures the above discussed metaphor of the 'core' of the right. That metaphor should not be taken to refer to a minimum amount of liberty that must be protected but to restricting liberty in a way that affects the two moral powers.

[45] For the criticism that Rawls's hypothetical contract is a redundant way to take into account the value of equality, see Dworkin R, *Taking Rights Seriously,* ch 6.

is necessary in order to establish the same scheme of equal basic liberties for all. In this latter case, the test of proportionality would be much easier because the liberties to be balanced are only the ones that are needed for the exercise of the two moral powers, rather than every liberty that is part of a protected interest as the interest-based model implies. As Rawls notes, 'if there are many basic liberties, their specification into a coherent scheme securing the central range of application of each may prove too cumbersome. This leads us to ask what are the truly fundamental cases and to introduce a criterion of significance of a particular right or liberty'.[46]

It is also important to note that Rawls does not describe the distributional principle (the second principle of justice) in terms of rights and liberties as he does for the first principle, but in an impersonal sense ('social and economic inequalities are to be arranged . . .'). Yet while he calls the first principle the 'liberty principle', it turns out that the value in play is not liberty but the two moral powers. Why can't we say then that there is a right to those benefits or opportunities that work to the greatest benefit of the least advantaged? Or that the liberty of the least advantaged is restricted when the difference principle is violated and that courts can judicially protect it?

I think the explanation lies in that Rawls thinks of the first principle as referring to rights and liberties that are to be protected by courts. For he notes that the difference principle should not be affirmed in the constitution, nor should judges have the power to enforce it because 'this task is not one they can perform well'.[47] It seems to me clear that Rawls recognizes the conceptual link between the anti-utilitarian and anti-perfectionist role of rights on one hand and their judicial protection on the other. [48]

Dworkin's Rights as Trumps

Dworkin's theory of rights has been extremely influential among liberals and human rights advocates for its distinctive anti-utilitarian character. Yet his

---

[46] *Justice as Fairness: A Restatement*, at 112.

[47] ibid at 162.

[48] This is not to say, however, that Rawls opposes the judicial protection of social and economic rights. On the contrary, he argues that the liberty principle 'may be preceded by a lexically prior principle requiring that basic needs are met, at least insofar as their being met is a necessary condition for citizens to understand and to be able fruitfully to exercise the basic rights and liberties'. ibid at 44. He adds that this social minimum covering the basic needs should be a constitutional essential 'for it is reasonably obvious that the difference principle is rather blatantly violated when that minimum is not guaranteed'. This echoes the 'minimum core' approach to social and economic rights found in international human rights law. On this appraoch see CESCR, General Comment 3, 'The Nature of States Parties Obligations', 14/12/90. For a detailed analysis of art 2(1) ICESCR and of General Comment No 3 see Craven M, *The International Covenant on Economic, Social and Cultural Rights: A Perspective on its Development* (Oxford University Press 1995) pp 106–52.

slogan that rights are trumps has been widely misunderstood,[49] so it is worth discussing it in some detail.

Dworkin's philosophy is premised on a very distinctive account of the values of liberty and equality. Traditionally, people thought that the values of liberty and equality necessarily conflict: the more we try to make people equal the more we have to restrict their liberty. This conflict between liberty and equality has often been used to signal the differences between right wing and left wing politics. Libertarians view the welfare state as an intrusion on liberty whereas egalitarians view laissez-faire capitalism and the minimal state as the cause of great social inequalities. It is a fundamental aspect of Dworkin's philosophy that liberty and equality are not distinct political values that are in competition. This is part of his broader moral and political philosophy, inspired by the idea that we should try to construe the important values of our political morality, not in isolation, but each in the light of the other.[50]

Equality, in Dworkin's view, may seem to conflict with liberty only on a certain interpretation of liberty found in the tradition of Isaiah Berlin and his influential idea of negative liberty. This is the idea that liberty is diminished whenever individuals are obstructed from pursuing a certain activity, whatever this activity may be. Negative liberty is limited whenever someone is prevented from speaking, walking, or exercising his or her religion, but it is also diminished whenever he or she is prevented from murdering, defaming others, visiting Mars, or having more than a fair share of resources.

In *Taking Rights Seriously*, Dworkin argued that this conception of liberty and a corresponding general right to liberty are misleading.[51] We seem to value liberty not in the sense of being able to do everything that it is possible for one to do, but in the sense of being able to exercise important, or basic, liberties. For there are liberties that are diminished every day in a number of ways, yet we do not feel that something is thereby lost or that we have a *right* to those liberties. We would not say, Dworkin argues, that we have a right to drive up Lexington Avenue if the government decides to make it one way downtown. But although we find it unproblematic that we are prevented from driving up Lexington Avenue, we would find it deeply illiberal if some people, whose views the majority disagrees with, are not allowed to speak freely.

Now, the distinction between basic and trivial liberties cannot be made, Dworkin claims, on the basis that people just happen to want basic liberties

---

[49] See the exchange between Waldron and Pildes above.

[50] See also, Dworkin R, 'Hart's Postscript and the Character of Political Philosophy' 24(1) *Oxford Journal of Legal Studies* (2004) 1.

[51] 'Indeed it seems to me absurd to suppose that men and women have any general right to liberty at all, at least as liberty has traditionally been conceived by its champions' in Dworkin R, *Taking Rights Seriously*, at 267.

more than other liberties. For there are people who are more frustrated by the restrictions on movement imposed by the traffic code, for instance, than by restrictions on political speech. The distinction therefore, Dworkin claims, has to turn on the value that each liberty serves. He writes: 'if we have a right to basic liberties not because they are cases in which commodity of liberty is somehow especially at stake, but because an assault on basic liberties injures us or demeans us in some way that goes beyond its impact on liberty, then what we have a right to is not liberty at all, but to the values or interests or standing that this particular constraint defeats'.[52]

We discussed earlier in this chapter the idea that there is some value that distinguishes between important and trivial liberties. But in his early work Dworkin did not turn directly to what would seem the obvious candidate value here, namely, personal *autonomy* or *self-determination*. Instead, Dworkin invoked a fundamental right to *equal concern and respect*.

It is this right to equal respect and concern that Dworkin used as an objection to utilitarianism in *Taking Rights Seriously* and 'Rights as Trumps': utilitarianism fails to treat people as equals in violation of its own commitment to equality, ie to the Millian idea that each person should count as one and no person as more than one. We should not forget that utilitarianism emerged as a progressive theory that attacked aristocratic and other hereditary or class privileges. For utilitarianism, no one's preferences can be more important than the preferences of others. Yet, Dworkin argues, if utilitarianism allows *external* as well as personal preferences to enter into its calculation, then the practical outcome of the theory would amount to treating the preferences of some as more important than the preferences of others.

What are external preferences? External preferences can be said to be meta-preferences: they are not preferences for goods or opportunities that people want for themselves, but preferences about how other people's preferences should be treated while assigning goods or opportunities. Dworkin gives the example of the Sarah-lovers who prefer that Sarah's preferences count twice and the Nazi who prefers that Aryans have more and Jews less of their preferences fulfilled because of who they are. But if the preferences of Sarah-lovers are allowed in the utilitarian calculation then this, Dworkin claims, amounts to double-counting: Sarah's personal preferences will be counted twice, both in taking into account her personal preferences and in taking into account the (external) preferences of others. This, however, violates utilitarianism's

---

[52] The same idea is expressed in Dworkin R, *A Matter of Principle*, at 189: 'I do not mean that we can make no sense of the idea of fundamental liberties like freedom of speech. But we cannot argue in their favour by showing that they protect more liberty, taken to be an even roughly measurable commodity, than does the right to drive as we wish. The fundamental liberties are important because we value something else that they protect'.

fundamental egalitarian principle since it ends up treating the preferences of some as more important than those of others. Utilitarianism is a theory about how to treat people's preferences. If external preferences are also views about how to treat people's preferences, then they occupy the same conceptual level as utilitarianism itself. But at that level, they are inconsistent with utilitarianism's egalitarian principle and they have to be excluded from calculations.

Dworkin then proposed that in a society where utilitarianism operates as a background political justification, the inequality of counting external preferences can be remedied by introducing the idea of rights as trumps. Rights as trumps are relative to such a utilitarian 'package' of political justification:

> I wish now to propose the following general theory of rights. The concept of an individual right, in the strong anti-utilitarian sense I distinguished earlier, is a response to the philosophical defects of a utilitarianism that counts external preferences and the practical impossibility of a utilitarianism that does not. It allows us to enjoy the institutions of political democracy, which enforce overall or unrefined utilitarianism, and yet protect the fundamental right of citizens to equal concern and respect by prohibiting decisions that seem, antecedently, to have been reached by virtue of external components of the preferences democracy reveals.[53]

Dworkin thought that a society committed to utilitarianism as a general background justification may disqualify external preferences by adopting a right to moral independence, ie 'the right that no one suffer disadvantage in the distribution of goods or opportunities on the ground that others think he should have less because of who he is or is not or that others care less for him than they do for other people'. Traditional constitutional rights to free speech or freedom of religion block external preferences in areas (such as religion or speech) where we know that the utilitarian policies of our society are likely to contain external preferences and discriminate against some minority group. The right to free speech does not protect an interest that individuals have, nor does it isolate this interest from the demands of the common good. Rather, it aims to block policies enacted on the basis that some people should be deprived of their free speech or suffer in the exercise of their religion on the basis of who they are. But if someone is deprived of a liberty, for a reason other than a policy based on external preferences then no right has been violated. Rights as trumps, as Waldron correctly notes, do not protect fundamental interests of the individuals against the demands of the common good. Rather, they block reasons that are based on corrupted (or unrestricted) utilitarian calculations.[54]

---

[53] Dworkin R, *Taking Rights Seriously*, at 277.
[54] See Waldron J, 'Pildes on Dworkin's Theory of Rights' 29 *Journal of Legal Studies* (January 2000) 301–7.

In his early work Dworkin appeared hostile to the idea that rights may be grounded exclusively on autonomy and the interests that serve it.[55] He insisted that 'individual rights to distinct liberties must be recognised only when the fundamental right to treatment as an equal can be shown to require these rights'.[56] He used the same right to equal respect and concern as an argument for liberal neutrality: a government treats people as equals only if it is neutral towards their conception of the good life. [57]

We can summarize Dworkin's early theory of rights as trumps in the following way: it is not the case that people have a right to specific liberties such as speech, religion, or assembly; rather, that they have a right not to be deprived of a liberty on the basis that their conception of the good life is inferior. Specific rights therefore exist only when, and to the extent that, there are liberties of individuals that the majority is likely to attack motivated by hostile external preferences. Freedom of speech, freedom of religion, and due process have become especially protected rights, not because religion or speech are important but because prejudiced majorities usually choose to attack these particular individual liberties. Dworkin argues moreover that this theory of rights best captures the way rights function within the United States constitutional framework.[58] Restricting freedom of contract in the famous *Lochner* case was not a violation of rights because it was based on welfare policies and not hostile external preferences.[59] And women have a right to an abortion, not because they have an interest in controlling their physical body but because prohibition is based on religious reasons about the sanctity of fetal life.[60]

Now Dworkin's attempt to derive rights from an egalitarian objection to (unrestricted) utilitarianism was criticized by HLA Hart.[61] Hart objected

[55] He writes: 'These different objections are plainly connected because they suppose that whatever rights people have are at least in large part timeless rights necessary to protect enduring and important interests fixed by human nature and fundamental to human development, like interests in the choice of sexual partners and acts and choice of religious conviction. That is a familiar theory of what rights are and what they are for, and I said that I would not give my reasons, in this essay, for thinking that it is in the end an inadequate theory of rights', in Dworkin R, 'Rights as Trumps', at 164.

[56] Dworkin R, *Taking Rights Seriously*, at 273–4.

[57] 'Since the citizens of a society differ in their conceptions, the government does not treat them as equals if it prefers one conception over another, either because the officials believe that one is intrinsically superior, or because it is held by the more numerous or more powerful group.' Dworkin R, *A Matter of Principle*, at 191.

[58] Ironically, Richard Pildes also uses some of the US Supreme Court decisions to support a reason-blocking theory of rights that he erroneously thinks is the opposite of Dworkin's rights as trumps. See Pildes R, 'Why Rights Are Not Trumps: Social Meanings, Expressive Harms, and Constitutionalism' 17 *Journal of Legal Studies* (June 1998) 725.

[59] *Taking Rights Seriously*, at 276.

[60] See Dworkin R, *Life's Dominion* (1993) at 154–68.

[61] See his 'Between Utility and Rights' in Hart HLA, *Essays in Jurisprudence and Philosophy* (1983) at 208.

that counting the *favourable* external preferences of the Sarah-lovers does not amount to double-counting but that, on the contrary, disregarding their preferences would fail to treat them as equals. More crucially, he noted that when someone is deprived of a liberty or an opportunity on the basis of who he or she is (hostile external preferences), no double-counting is involved. Dworkin's argument that hostile external preferences do not treat people as equals is not, Hart argued, an internal objection to the fairness of the utilitarian process. Rather, the argument presupposes the substantive view that it is generally wrong to deprive people of liberty or opportunity on the basis that we despise or have contempt for their way of life. Hart writes:

The objection is no longer that the utilitarian argument or majority vote, is, like double counting, unfair as a procedure because it counts 'external preferences', but that a particular upshot of the procedure where the balance is tipped by a particular kind of external preferences, one which denies liberty and is assumed to express contempt, fails to treat people as equals. But this is a vice not of the mere externality of the preferences that have tipped the balance but of their content: that is, the liberty-denying and respect-denying content. But this is no longer to assign certain liberties the status of ('anti-utilitarian') rights simply as a response to the specific defects of utilitarianism as Dworkin claims to do.[62]

In his response to Hart, Dworkin argued that disregarding the favourable external preferences of the Sarah-lovers is not unfair because, unlike the case of votes, their personal preferences are still entered into the utilitarian computer. Blocking their external preferences does not affect the fulfilment of their personal preferences, Dworkin claimed, because by reporting their preference for Sarah's success, they do not have any less for themselves.

There are some difficulties with Dworkin's response, as both Sarah's success and the Sarah-lovers' personal preferences would depend on resources that are limited. Indeed, by reporting their preference for Sarah's success they do limit the resources available for the fulfilment of their personal preferences. Their favourable external preference may well affect the fulfilment of their other personal preferences, which is something they might be fully aware of and accept.[63] Disregarding their favourable external preference would then logically amount to disregarding their preferences altogether and hence not treating them as equals.[64]

[62] 'Between Utility and Rights' in Hart's *Essays in Jurisprudence and Philosophy* at 217

[63] Recall Nozick's famous Will Chamberlain example in his *Anarchy, State and Utopia* (1974), at ch 7: people may choose to be made worse off by paying money to see Will Chamberlain playing. They have a preference for his success that dramatically affects the fulfilment of their personal preferences. Would allowing this amount to double-counting? I think not and I fail to see the difference between this example and Dworkin's Sarah-lovers.

[64] Of course, the end result of counting external preferences may well be that the personal preferences of the much-loved Sarah are fulfilled at the expense of the personal preferences of the

But what is important is that Dworkin agreed with Hart that in cases of hostile external preferences, the problem lies not in the fact that the preferences are external, but in the content of the justification given. He writes: 'it is exactly that the minority must suffer because others find the lives they propose to lead disgusting, which seems no more justifiable, in a society committed to treating people as equals than the proposition we earlier considered and rejected, as incompatible with equality, that some people must suffer disadvantage under the law because others do not like them'.[65]

Indeed in Dworkin's later writings on equality, the right of moral independence is not derived from an egalitarian objection to utilitarianism but from what he calls the principle of special responsibility. This principle insists that 'so far as choices are to be made about the kind of life a person lives, within whatever range of choice is permitted by resource and culture, he is responsible for making those choices himself'.[66] Traditional constitutional liberties moreover are seen in *Sovereign Virtue* as having a separate justification in their role in distributive justice. Dworkin argues that it makes no sense to say that we need an objective list of goods or opportunities in order to choose and pursue a conception of a good life, without taking into account the amount of resources that it is fair for us to have.[67] Instead of equality of welfare he advances a theory of equality of resources using the device of a hypothetical auction and insurance scheme and argues that traditional constitutional liberties would be essential for achieving equality of resources through the auction scheme: if someone cannot know what use she will make of the resources she is bidding for in the auction, she will be unable to set her bidding priorities.[68] Traditional civil and political rights are essential for equality of resources, over and above the idea that they should not be restricted on the basis of external preferences.

It is important however to highlight that this argument (that the equality of resources would require the traditional constitutional rights) differs from an interest-based theory of rights. The argument is not that the well-being of persons depends on these rights. Rather, the connection is normative: using the idea of an auction scheme would be unfair if people do not know what use

---

majority. It may therefore seem that a minority will end up having more of its preferences fulfilled than the majority. But this is hardly an accurate description, if the majority (say, the Sarah-lovers) is willing to sacrifice significantly their own preferences for the sake of the personal preferences of some minority. Why would they not have a right to sacrifice their own preferences? It seems to me that favourable external preferences are not meta-preferences and do not occupy the same conceptual level as utilitarianism itself.

[65] Dworkin R, 'Rights as trumps' in Waldron J (ed) *Theories of Rights* (1984) at 161.
[66] Dworkin R, *Sovereign Virtue*, p 6.
[67] Dworkin R, *Sovereign Virtue*, at chs 1 and 2.
[68] Dworkin R, *Sovereign Virtue*, at ch 3.

they can make of the resources they bid for. This is why Dworkin notes that we should not expect most people to value protection of those rights more than they value promotion of their other interests.[69] In a world where resources are scarce, people may care more about having a better health system than being allowed to participate in large and unpopular demonstrations that require heavy policing.

Liberal Egalitarian Principles for the Interpretation of the Limitation Clauses

We should now draw some valuable conclusions from the preceding discussion of Rawls and Dworkin. The first is that there should be no direct inference from the interests and well-being of persons to what rights they have. The role of traditional civil rights, like freedom of thought, free speech, or right to private life, is not to maximize or improve the well-being of people. The second and related conclusion is that rights play a role as constraints to what *the government* may do. They flow from the duty of political communities to treat their members as equals. It is wrong therefore to complain about a violation of rights outside the context of governmental acts or omissions.[70]

Thirdly, we have a fundamental right not to be deprived of any liberty or opportunity on the basis of certain considerations: that our plan of life is impoverished or immoral; that we are despised by the majority; that our views shock and offend others; that we should be forced to lead a particular kind of life; and that our life is worth less than the life of others. Rights thus understood are *absolute*: it can never become justified for the government to restrict my liberty for the reasons[71] just mentioned. When these reasons are present, balancing is morally inappropriate. When these reasons are absent, we should not say that we have a right which is not absolute and whose limitation is justified. Rather, we should say that we had no right in the first place.

[69] Dworkin R, *Sovereign Virtue*, at 137.

[70] That is not to say that civil rights are only negative. They may well require positive action. But the duty holder must always be the state. For a discussion on the act/omission distinction in the context of human rights adjudication, see Nino C, *The Ethics of Human Rights,* at 195. Note that standard international human rights law cases of positive obligations, in which state failure to prevent or investigate into force disappearances is declared a violation of the right to life, involve hostile external preferences of the government towards members of a dissident political movement. See *Velazquez Rodriguez v Honduras* Series C No 4 I/A Court HR, Judgment of July 29. On duties of investigation under the ECHR see Mowbray A, 'Duties of Investigation Under the European Convention on Human Rights' 51 *International and Comparative Law Quarterly* (2002) 437.

[71] I should note that according to a certain philosophical tradition about reasons, impermissable considerations of the kind that liberal rights block do not constitue reasons in the first place. They are simply false normative beliefs that do not justify any action. According to this tradition, it would be misleading to say that rights block *reasons* since the government has no reason to do any of the things that rights prohibit.

Consider Holmes's famous example: nobody has a right to shout falsely 'fire' in a crowded theatre.[72] We do not have a right to act in a way that creates a clear and present danger for the life of others.

Fourthly, some civil rights, like freedom of speech, freedom of thought, and freedom of association, have a special normative role. They are important for our status as free and equal citizens who are responsible for choosing and pursuing a conception of the good life. They are also important for the values of democracy and social justice: the legitimacy of the outcome of an election and of how resources are distributed depends on these rights. It is therefore important to ensure that these liberties are not limited for *speculative* or *marginal* benefits to the interests of others when they do play these normative roles. It causes great inconvenience to allow demonstrations on a regular basis in the city centre. But unless they pose a clear and present danger to the lives of others then they should not be banned because they are justified by their democratic role. If, however, there is a clear and present danger to vital interests of others, such as their life and physical integrity, then no right is violated by restricting liberty. There is nothing wrong with using a consequentialist test to establish the existence of a clear and present danger. Rights are anti-utilitarian, not anti-consequentialist.[73] By contrast, the government may routinely restrict liberty when it does not engage the above values, even for speculative or marginal benefits. It may introduce a congestion charge for driving to the city centre and cause great inconvenience to most of us, on the grounds that it might improve the aesthetics of the city. Such policy would be naïve or extravagant but it would not be a violation of human rights.

Fifthly, the above principles and the role they assign to civil rights are to some extent tailored to their judicial protection by courts. As I mentioned in Chapter 1, we can use the vocabulary of rights to state many valuable moral goals that the government has a reason to promote. But when courts have the authority to assess the validity of any legal norm against abstract moral standards, there must be some independent reason why courts are more likely than legislatures to get these moral standards right.

Of course it does not follow logically from the liberal principles above that courts, rather than some other institutional body, should have the power to

---

[72] 'The most stringent protection of free speech would not protect a man in falsely shouting fire in a theatre and causing a panic', in *Schenck v US*, 249 US 47 (1919). Dworkin remarked to me in conversation that it is crucial in Holmes's example that someone *falsely* shouts 'fire!'. For we do have a right to shout 'fire!' in a crowded theatre when there is actually a fire.

[73] Utilitarianism is one variant of consequentialism, which is distinguished by how it measures the goodness of the consequences and its distribution across persons. Not all consequentialist theories are utilitarian. All moral theories moreover take consequences into account. Even Immanuel Kant, who is taken to be the archetypical deontologist, employed consequentialist reasoning; see Cummiskey D, 'Kantian Consequentialism' 100 *Ethics* (1990) 586.

decide on the appropriate content and limits of rights.[74] Who gets to decide on human rights issues must to some extent depend on who has more chances of reaching the right answer. Such considerations are particularly relevant when the question is how to construct from a scratch a system of human rights protection that can be viable and effective given the various social and political circumstances.[75] In the long run, courts may produce decisions that restrict fundamental rights rather than protect them, in which case there is a strong reason to reconsider allowing them the power of judicial review. Yet it is natural to assume that courts will normally reach better decisions than legislatures. Given that rights have an anti-majoritarian dimension, it makes no sense to allow the majority itself to decide what rights individuals have in controversial legal cases. Historically, political majorities have had it in their interest to restrict the rights of unpopular groups. But this is more than an appeal to history—it further reflects the general moral principle that no one should be judge of his own cause. If we insist that the majority must respect individual rights, we cannot then ask the majority itself to decide whether it has indeed respected them. For it is natural to assume that the majority will often judge itself to have done so, even when this is not the case.

---

[74] This point is made in detail by Sadurski W, 'Judicial Review and the Protection of Constitutional Rights' 22 *Oxford Journal of Legal Studies* (2002) 275. The leading critic of courts having the power of judicial review is Jeremy Waldron. See Waldron J, 'A Right-Based Critique of Constitutional Rights' 13 *Oxford Journal of Legal Studies* (1993) 18. See also Waldron J, *Law and Disagreement* (1999) at 232–54 and Waldron J, 'The Core of the Case Against Judicial Review' 115 *Yale Law Journal* (2006) 1346.

[75] For an in-depth comparative analysis of bills of rights, discussing arguments for and against constitutional entrenchment, see Darrow M and Alston P, 'Bills of Rights in Comparative Perspective' in Alston (ed) *Promoting Human Rights Through Bills of Rights* (1999) 465.

6

Public Morals, Consensus, and Rights Inflation: A Critique

Introduction

In this final chapter I return to the case law on the margin of appreciation, which I assess in the light of the liberal principles of human rights interpretation that were highlighted in the previous chapter. I shall discuss three categories of cases. The first comprises cases where the Court took the moralistic preferences of the majority to constitute a legitimate aim for interfering with a Convention right under the term 'public morals' in the limitation clauses. The second comprises cases in which the Court's judgment turned, to a lesser or greater degree, on whether there is a consensus among Contracting States. Both these categories belong to the use of the margin of appreciation that I termed structural: the margin of appreciation is invoked in relation to the status of the ECtHR as an international court and of the ECHR as an international treaty. The third category comprises cases which balance various welfare interests against collective goals, in relation to which states are said to have a 'wide margin of appreciation'. This latter category belongs to what I called the substantive use of the margin of appreciation, namely, cases that the Court takes to be about the appropriate limits of state interference with Convention rights in articles that have limitation clauses. My aim is to criticize the arguments that are entailed or presupposed by these judgments, drawing on liberal principles of human rights.

Public Morals and the Moralistic Preferences of the Majority

Recall that what I called the structural concept of the margin of appreciation figures mainly in cases involving 'private sphere rights', under arts 8 (right to private and family life), 9 (freedom of religion), 10 (freedom of expression), and 14 (prohibition of discrimination) ECHR. The Court's standard approach in these cases has been that the less consensus there is among Contracting States on the human rights issue raised by the applicant, the better placed the national authorities are to decide on it and the more deferential the Court should be towards them in its final judgment. Put differently, the more weight the Court feels it has to put on the decision of the national authorities owing to the lack of consensus, the wider the margin of appreciation that state is said to enjoy.

Deference on the basis of consensus violates the liberal principles I highlighted in the previous chapter. This is because consensus in each Contracting State—and across Contracting States generally—is bound to contain hostile external preferences. Consider the cases discussed in Chapter 4: confiscation and seizure of obscene books (*Handyside*) or paintings (*Muller*), confiscation and seizure of films (*Otto-Preminger-Institut*), and paintings (*Wingrove*) that offend the dominant religion, prohibition on advertisement of unpopular religions (*Murphy*), refusal to recognize the new gender identity of post-operation transsexuals (*Rees, Sheffield and Horsham*), and refusal to grant adoption rights to homosexuals (*Frette*). All these instances involve the moralistic preferences of the majority, ie its external preference that some people should not enjoy some liberty on the basis that their plan of life is inferior. People who enjoy books with sexual advice or erotic art should be deprived of this liberty because pornography or erotic art is considered degrading by the majority. People who are atheists or believe in unpopular religions should not have the right to express themselves or advertise their religious views because their views offend the religious beliefs of the majority. People who have a sex operation should not be granted legal recognition of their new gender because change of sex offends the institution of marriage. People who are in a homosexual relationship and wish to adopt should not be allowed this liberty because the majority despises homosexual families and the adopted children will suffer from this prejudice.

It is clear moreover that in these cases the Court takes the moralistic preferences of the majority as being synonymous with 'public morals' and thus constituting a legitimate aim. In fact, the Court's early view in *Handyside*, *The Sunday Times* and *Muller* was that they should defer to the judgment of national authorities because they are in a better position to know what the moralistic preferences of the majority are and what restrictions they call for. The idea was that requirements of morals vary from place to place and from time to time and state authorities are better placed to define and apply these requirements 'by reason of their direct and continuous contact with the vital forces of their countries'. Needless to say, no plausible theory of human rights, at least one with liberal-egalitarian aspirations, would ever allow moralistic preferences to constitute a legitimate restriction on liberty.[1] To call

---

[1] This goes back to the famous debate in the United Kingdom between Lord Devlin and HLA Hart on the criminal enforcement of morals. See Hart HLA, *Law, Liberty and Morality* (1963) and Devlin P, *The Enforcement of Morals* (1965).

the moralistic preferences of the majority the 'vital forces of the country' is the greatest insult to values of liberty and equality. No one has the right to impose his or her own ethical beliefs on others, or coerce others into abandoning their ethical views on the basis that they are inferior or degrading. The Court is therefore wrong to hold that there is a right not to be insulted in one's religious feelings by the public expression of views of other persons.[2] Rights *block* moralistic preferences; they do not give effect to them.

It may be objected that the Court is bound to take moralistic preferences into account, in violation of liberal principles, simply because the term 'public morals' figures in the list of legitimate aims in the limitation clauses. However, this textualist interpretation of the accommodation clauses cannot save the argument from consensus. Nothing about the word 'public morals' necessitates this interpretation. As we saw in Chapter 3, textualism as a theory of interpretation must be based on the attribution of substantive value to that which is interpreted in order to get off the ground. Besides, we can very easily attribute a different meaning to this concept, one that coheres with the moral principles that underlie rights. As Christopher Nowlin[3] notes aptly, 'public morals' could be interpreted as referring to what Hart called *critical* as opposed to *communal* morality.[4] Given that the enforcement of communal morality violates the liberal principles of human rights, then reference in the Convention to protecting public morals 'must be construed to mean respect for the moral rights of others, and proper judicial attention to these rights should always render moral majoritarianism or legal moralism suspect in civil and human rights analyses'. [5]

It seems that the Court has never actually questioned the meaning it attributes to public morals in the accommodation clauses. Deference was justified on the basis that national authorities are better placed to construe and enforce the requirements of communal morality, particularly in the absence of a uniform conception of morals in the Contracting States. It should now be apparent that the question is not who is in a better position to interpret the requirements of communal morality or whether Contracting States share the same communal morality. Allowing the requirements of communal morality to limit rights, either through the Court's own interpretation or by deferring to the judgment of national authorities, violates the moral values of human rights. The moralistic preferences of the majority as to what liberties people should be free to enjoy cannot constitute a legitimate aim for interfering with

---

[2] *Wingrove v UK*, paras 45–48.

[3] Nowlin C, 'The Protection of Morals Under the European Convention for the Protection of Human Rights and Fundamental Freedoms', 24 *Human Rights Quarterly* (2002) 264.

[4] Hart HLA, *Law, Liberty and Morality*, at 20.

[5] Nowlin C, 'The Protection of Morals Under the European Convention', at 286.

a Convention right. When they are in play, they should be blocked rather than balanced against the applicant's right. Proportionality there has no role to play.

Consensus, Piecemeal Evolution, and Legality

Apart from its role in the interpretation of the term 'public morals', consensus has played another role in the jurisprudence of the Court. Recall the case law on the rights of transsexuals. In 1986, the Court said that there was at that time 'little common ground among Contracting States in this area' and that 'accordingly this is an area in which the Contracting States enjoy a wide margin of appreciation'.[6] In 1990, the Court noted that there had been some developments in the law of some of the Member States but held that the same diversity of practice existed as existed four years earlier.[7] In 1998, it repeated, despite legal developments, that there was no common European approach to the problems created by the recognition in law of post-operative gender status.[8] In 2002, 16 years after its first judgment, the Court reversed its case law and declared a violation, on the basis that in present-day conditions there is an evolving convergence within Contracting States as to the standards to be achieved.[9]

Recall that present-day conditions, as an interpretative principle, figures in the Court's 'evolutive' interpretation, or 'living instrument' approach. This method may be viewed as updating the Convention standards according to what the majority of Contracting States believe at each given time.[10] This idea differs from the argument that each country should be left free to use its public morals as a legitimate restriction on rights. Rather, the idea seems to be that the Court should wait for a consensus within Contracting States to be established, before it rules something to be a violation. This is because it is felt that the Court should not rush into finding the majority of states in breach of the Convention whenever there is a new evolving standard. Rather, it should first warn them that a new standard is evolving and allow them time to reform their policies gradually, in line with present-day conditions.[11]

Is this argument valid? Benvenisti notes that the argument is flawed because it can only draw its justification from 19th-century theories of state

---

[6] *Rees v United Kingdom*, para 37.
[7] *Cossey v United Kingdom*, para 234.
[8] *Sheffield and Horsham v United Kingdom*, paras 57–58.
[9] *Goodwin v United Kingdom*, para 74.
[10] See the discussion in ch 3.
[11] See Helfer L and Slaughter AM, 'Toward a Theory of Effective Supranational Adjudication' 107 *Yale Law Journal* (1997) 317. See also Benvenisti E, 'Margin of Appreciation, Consensus and Universal Standards' 31 *New York Journal of International Law and Politics* (1998–1999), 851.

consent[12] and the view that states can only be bound either through their own consent or through the notion of an emerging custom. On this view, each and every violation of an ECHR right must meet the criteria of customary international law within Contracting States for the Court to declare it. As we saw in Chapter 1, this view is flawed as a general thesis about international legal duties. But it is even more problematic in the case of the ECHR. Member States agreed in the aftermath of the Second World War to undertake the legal obligation towards their own people to respect human rights; they did not undertake the obligation to respect what, at each given time, most of them take these rights to be.

There is moreover a further difficulty with the idea of a piecemeal evolution. ECHR rights are legal rights that condition when the use of coercion by Member States is legitimate. Legality insists that the benefit of the moral principles that justify these rights must be extended equally to all. If Europeans have the right to marry their heterosexual partner or practise their sexual preference without criminal prosecution, then the applicants in *Rees, Cossey* and *Sheffield* also had the right to have their birth certificates changed so that they can get married. For the same moral principle justifies both rights, namely that no one should be deprived of a liberty or an opportunity on the basis that others despise his or her way of life. By denying them this right, the European Court of Human Rights treated the applicants in an unprincipled manner. For 16 years, until the Court reversed its case law in 2002, some people (like the applicant in *Dudgeon*) could rely on the European Court to benefit from this moral principle but others (like the applicants in *Rees, Cossey* and *Sheffield)* could not. Piecemeal evolution of the ECHR standards according to how many states have abandoned moralistic preferences in different areas of national law deeply offends the values of legality and equality.

But could there be a moral principle that can be attributed to the ECHR and justify the idea of a consensus-based piecemeal evolution? It may be argued that deference must sometimes be justified because the European Court risks losing its authority if it reaches decisions that are unpopular in the majority of Contracting States. If the Court does not wait for a consensus to be established there is a danger—the argument goes—that the Court's judgments will be ignored altogether or, worse, that some Contracting States will withdraw from the ECHR. As a consequence, the protection of human rights in Europe will suffer as, surely, it is better to have a gradual improvement of human rights protection than none at all. The moral values of human rights cannot be insensitive to the number of violations that can be prevented. As Benvenisti notes, however, the above argument is based on an overstated fear.[13] For even if the Court

[12] Benvenisti E, 'Margin of Appreciation', at 852.
[13] Benvenisti E, 'Margin of Appreciation', at 851–2.

lacked authority in its early years, the institutional majority of the Member States, imperfect as it may be, would hardly justify this fear now. The Court has earned respect and recognition at both national and international levels.

But what about the new Member States? Many of the new ECHR members from Eastern Europe have a poor human rights record, a fragile rule of law, and an unstable political system. These states may struggle to solve all these problems at once and human rights violations ruled by Strasbourg may frustrate them and force them to distance themselves from the Council of Europe and its goals. Some commentators note that the new Eastern European Member States are unable to meet minimum standards of human rights protection (among other things, owing to their economic and political situation) and that the Court will inevitably use the margin of appreciation doctrine to 'lower its standards'.[14]

Two points can be made in response. The first is that most of the cases in which consensus was used as an interpretative principle came from the old ECHR Members to which none of these considerations applies. The second point is that, as I argued in Chapter 5, we should be sceptical of the idea of 'minimum standards' of human rights protection. Protecting human rights as *legal* rights is not a matter of maximizing or increasing the amount to which certain individual interests are served. It is a matter of applying consistently the moral principles that underlie rights, to how state coercion is used.

That is not to say, however, that extreme circumstances in Member States should never be taken into account, that the European Court should respect legality and apply coherently human rights principles whatever the consequences. As in municipal law, a judge's moral duties are not exhausted by his or her duty to apply the law.[15] If there is a clear and present danger that the ruling of a violation will trigger political turmoil and violence that will directly harm important interests of the people in the respondent state, then the Court is morally justified in ignoring the law and granting a margin of appreciation. Note that this argument is not based at all on cultural relativism or the idea that the cultural particularities of the various Member States should be respected. It is a consequentialist argument with which the values of human rights and legality are perfectly comfortable.

It is important to stress, however, that such exceptional cases should be extremely rare. Perhaps one example can be found in cases coming from Turkey on the dissolution of extremist Islamist parties[16] and the prohibition

---

[14] See Bowring B, 'Russia's Accession to the Council of Europe and Human Rights: Compliance or Cross-Purposes' 6 *European Human Rights Law Review* (1997) 628–43. On the reception of the ECHR in Russia see Kahn JD, 'Russia's "Dictatorship of Law" and the European Court of Human Rights' 29 *Review of Central and East European Law* (2004) 1.

[15] See Dworkin's distinction between the grounds and the force of law in *Law's Empire*, pp 110–111.

[16] See *Refah Partisi (The Welfare Party) and Others v Turkey* (Grand Chamber), Judgment of 13 February 2003, Reports 2003-II.

on wearing the headscarf.[17] In *Leyla Sahin* the European Court had to rule on whether the prohibition 'to cover the neck and hair with a veil or head-scarf for reasons of religious conviction' in Turkish universities amounted to a violation of freedom of expression. In the chamber judgment, the Court invoked the margin of appreciation doctrine and reiterated the view that lack of consensus among Contracting States is a basis for deference:

A margin of appreciation is particularly appropriate when it comes to the regulation by the Contracting States of the wearing of religious symbols in teaching institutions, since rules on the subject vary from one country to another depending on national traditions and there is no uniform European conception of the requirements of 'the protection of the rights of others' and of 'public order'.[18]

This view, as I argued above, does not constitute a justified basis for deference. It cannot be the case that the prohibition to wear a headscarf is justified because there is no uniform European conception of the proper role of religion. But this was not the actual basis for the Court's ruling that there was no breach of the ECHR. The Court pointed to the link between promoting secularism and maintaining democracy in a country where the majority of the population adhere to the Islamic faith, the idea being that measures restricting the expression of religious beliefs in public are necessary in order to maintain a democratic system and the separation of state and religion in Turkey. The Court said explic-itly that 'it did not lose sight of the fact that there were extremist political move-ments in Turkey which sought to impose on society as a whole their religious symbols and conception of a society founded on religious precepts'.[19]

I believe that allowing Turkey a margin of appreciation in this case had nothing to do with respecting cultural differences or waiting for a consen-sus to be formed regarding restrictions on wearing religious symbols at uni-versities. The argument was that these restrictions were necessary in order to protect a democratic and secular political regime which is at risk. There is nothing wrong in principle about this argument, and the Court's assessment about whether such restrictions are necessary should be cautious. But as I said, such cases should be rare and should not obscure the fact that the moral principles behind the ECHR rights are universal and objective.

Rights Inflation: *Hatton* and the Right to Sleep Well

How many rights do we have? Are we better off the more we have? I men-tioned in Chapter 5 that many believe that the point of civil rights is to protect

---

[17] *Leyla Şahin v Turkey*, Judgment of 29 June 2004 (Chamber).
[18] ibid para 102.
[19] ibid para 109.

interests that can be served in varying degrees and that what human rights courts do is to set the threshold of their protection as a matter of law of the ECHR. I argued against this belief on the grounds that it fails to capture the morality of rights and their role as legal rights which courts have a duty to enforce against the government. I also argued that we do not have a right to anything but only a right not to be deprived of certain liberties for certain reasons and that rights thus understood are always absolute.

Yet in the practice of the ECtHR one finds numerous examples where the Court examines whether a particular policy has struck a fair balance between various interests, none of which relate to the values I highlighted earlier as supporting traditional civil rights, namely, the responsibility one has for the success of his own life and the value of democracy. There is a trend to read various welfare interests into that which the rights of the ECHR are rights to, inviting the Court to assess whether a Member State's policy disproportionately affects them. The Court usually declares such cases admissible and in its assessment it often refers to the substantive concept of the margin of appreciation, ie the view that if an interference with a convention right is proportionate, the respondent state acted within the margin, and if it is disproportionate, the state overstepped the margin.

No doubt this trend has generated an inflation of human rights claims and increased the caseload of the European Court. The best example of this trend is found in the *Hatton* case.[20] The applicants in this case were residents near Heathrow airport in London, and were complaining about the level of noise caused by a new scheme of night flights. The Chamber judgment ruled this to be a violation but the Grand Chamber later reversed it. It is worth discussing the two judgments in some detail to highlight the problems with the inflation of rights.

The applicants in *Hatton* submitted that the sleep disturbance, distress, and ill health caused by night flights at Heathrow airport was a violation of their right to private life under art 8 ECHR. The UK Government responded that the central issue had to do with striking a fair and reasonable balance between the various interests involved, in particular, the economic well-being of the United Kingdom on the one hand, and the private life interests of local residents on the other. It claimed that 'it was not possible to separate the economic importance of night flights at Heathrow from the overall importance of Heathrow to the United Kingdom economy' and that the balance struck was fair and reasonable.[21]

In its chamber judgment, the ECtHR noted that 'mere reference to the economic well-being of the country is not sufficient to outweigh the rights

[20] *Hatton and Others v United Kingdom*, Grand Chamber judgment of 8 July 2003, unreported.
[21] *Hatton v United Kingdom*, Judgment of 2 October 2001, para 90.

of others' and that 'states are required to minimise, as far as possible, the interference with these rights, by trying to find alternative solutions and by generally seeking to achieve their aims in the least onerous way as regards human rights'.[22] It then went on to note that there was no detailed assessment by the government of the exact contribution of night flights to the economy nor any serious evaluation of the impact that night flights have on the applicants' sleep. This was enough for the Chamber to find a violation. Following a request by the UK Government, the case was subsequently referred to the Grand Chamber of the European Court of Human Rights.

The Grand Chamber reiterated its position that states generally enjoy a wide margin of appreciation in environmental and planning issues but that this margin is reduced in scope when government policy interferes with a particularly intimate aspect of an individual's life.[23] It then noted that it is faced with 'conflicting views' as to the margin of appreciation: 'on the one hand, the Government claim to a wide margin on the ground that the case concerns matters of general policy, and, on the other hand, the applicant's claim that where the ability to sleep is affected, the margin is narrow because of the "intimate" nature of the right protected'.[24]

The Court's subsequent analysis was dominated by the language of interests: the economic interests of the operators of airlines and other enterprises, the interests of travellers, the economic interests of the country as a whole, and the applicants' interest in avoiding sleep disturbance. It said that whether the right balance has been struck between art 8 ECHR and conflicting community interests depends on the relative weight to be given to each of them. It further examined whether the government had done anything to mitigate the effects of aircraft noise generally, and the procedural aspect of whether the scheme applied was based on investigations and studies aiming at striking a fair balance between the various conflicting interests. It concluded that the authorities had not overstepped their margin of appreciation, striking a fair balance between the right of individuals and the conflicting interests of others.

Despite the fact that no violation was ruled in the end, some serious objections can be raised against the Court's reasoning in both judgments. They both accepted the following two propositions: first, that someone's interest in sleep is part of the right to private life under art 8 ECHR, which competes with other people's interests in travelling and in having a healthy economy—both of which fall within the legitimate aims under the limitation clause of the same article; secondly, that the applicant's interest in sleep has relatively

---

[22] ibid para 97.
[23] *Hatton v United Kingdom*, Grand Chamber (2003), paras 101–2.
[24] ibid para 103.

more weight than the interests in travelling and in the economy, but can still be traded off against demands of the common good.

It is difficult to find principles that can support these two propositions. To be sure, we do have an interest to have a good night's sleep. But we also have an interest to eat well, to breathe clean air, to have medical care, to socialize with friends, to have a decent job and an income, to send our kids to a good school, to see good theatre, and many more. But do we have a legal right under the ECHR to all those things? It might be thought that the interest to sleep well is more fundamental than these other interests. But is it? Many of us I believe would rather live near Heathrow airport and learn to cope with the noise, if it meant better health care, better schools, and better income. After all, the applicants themselves could apparently cope with the noise. For there was no one stopping them from moving to another area. There was no financial dis-advantage either, as property prices in the area had not fallen since the night flight scheme was introduced.

It might be suggested that the interest to sleep well grounds a right because sleep is important no matter what one's plan of life is. But so is the interest to eat well, breathe clean air, and have a decent income. If we have a right to sleep well under the ECHR (qualified as it may be), then we also have a right under the ECHR to eat well, breathe clean air, and have a decent income. Principled consistency would require reading these rights into the ECHR too, inviting the European Court to decide when states have struck a fair balance.

I do not mean to imply that the distribution of noise and its effect on people's sleep in a society is not a concern of justice. Sleep can be seen as a resource that should be distributed in a society on an egalitarian basis. Perhaps the Heathrow night flights scheme did not allocate the various resources in play (sleep, economic benefits, employment) in a way that treats people as equals under some egalitarian theory of distribution. Perhaps the applicants have a solid claim based on distributive justice to request the government to restrict or abolish night flights, relocate the airport, or compensate the residents. But these are not matters falling within the law of human rights. We cannot inflate the concept of human rights so much that it covers the whole realm of justice. Human rights would then lose their distinctive moral force. As James Griffin remarks, freeriding offends justice and equality but it is not a violation of human rights.[25]

One often gets the impression that the European Court of Human Rights is willing to promote interests that are normally served by social and economic human rights (as political goals) but that can textually be read into the civil

---

[25] See Griffin J, 'Discrepancies Between the Best Philosophical Account of Human Rights and the International Law of Human Rights' 10 *Telos* (2001) 133.

rights of the ECHR.[26] This approach would be unjustified as it cannot be based on a moral principle whose benefit the Court extends to all. The Court's institutional responsibility is to interpret civil and political rights, not social and economic rights; the latter are governed by separate normative principles and form the subject matter of separate international treaties and monitoring bodies. Piecemeal and random promotion of welfare interests is not a mark of judicial innovation. It is a cause for concern over how seriously the Court takes the values of equality and legality.

Moreover, the idea that welfare interests are rights under the ECHR encourages the misleading picture that no right (apart from freedom from torture, slavery, and retrospective punishment) is absolute and that all rights must be balanced against collective goals. Here is how the Court compared the interpretative issue it faced in *Hatton* to that in *Dudgeon*:[27]

> The Court notes that the introduction of the 1993 Scheme for night flights was a general measure not specifically addressed to the applicants in this case, although it had obvious consequences for them and other persons in a similar situation. However, the sleep disturbances relied on by the applicants did not intrude into an aspect of private life in a manner comparable to that of the criminal measures considered in the case of Dudgeon to call for a narrow scope for the State's margin of appreciation.[28]

The Court correctly distinguishes between *Hatton* and the *Dudgeon* case in which criminalization of homosexuality in Northern Ireland was found to be in breach of art 8 ECHR. The latter is a case of imposing the moralistic preferences of a majority whereas the former is not. It is not that the government deprived Heathrow residents of their sleep on the grounds that their conception of the good life is inferior or that they should lead a particular kind of life. But the Court described this difference by saying that the margin of appreciation was narrow in *Dudgeon* and wide in *Hatton*. If we want to be accurate we have to say that in cases like *Hatton,* states' margin of appreciation is infinite and in cases like *Dudgeon* states have no margin of appreciation whatsoever.

---

[26] On the idea of the 'integrated approach' in the interpretation of civil rights see Mantouvalou V, 'Work and Private Life: Sidabras and Dziautas v Lithuania' 30(4) *European Law Review* (2005) 573.

[27] *Dudgeon v United Kingdom*, Judgment of 22 October 1981, Series A no 45.

[28] *Hatton v United Kingdom*, Grand Chamber (2003), para 123.

Bibliography

Arai-Takahashi Y, *The Margin of Appreciation Doctrine and the Principle of Proportionality in the Jurisprudence of the ECHR* (2002).

Beitz C, *Political Theory and International Relations* (1999, with afterword).

Benvenisti E, 'Margin of Appreciation, Consensus and Universal Standards' 31 *New York University Journal of International Law and Politics* (1998–1999) 843.

Bernhard R, 'The convention and domestic law' in Macdonald, Matscher, and Petzold (eds) *The European System for the Protection of Human Rights* (1993) 25.

——, 'Thoughts on the interpretation of human-rights treaties' in Matscher F, Petzfold H (eds) *Protecting Human Rights: the European Dimension* (1990) 65.

Blackburn S, 'Relativism' in LaFollete H (ed) *The Blackwell Companion to Ethical Thoery* (2000).

Bork R, *The Tempting of America* (1989).

Bowring B, 'Russia's Accession to the Council of Europe and Human Rights: Compliance or Cross-Purposes' 6 *European Human Rights Law Review* (1997) 628.

Brems E, 'The Margin of Appreciation Doctrine in the Case-law of the European Court of Human Rights' 56 *Zeitschrift für ausländisches öffentliches Recht und Völkerrecht* (1996) 240.

Brest P, 'The Misconceived Quest for the Original Understanding' 60 *Boston University Law Review* (1980) 204.

Brink, D, 'Legal Theory, Legal Interpretation and Judicial Review' 17 *Philosophy and Public Affairs* (1988) 105.

Burley J (ed) *Dworkin and His Critics* (2004).

Carozza P, 'Uses and Misuses of Comparative Law in International Human Rights: Some Reflections on the Jurisprudence of the European Court of Human Rights' 73 *Notre Dame Law Review* (1998) 1217.

Cassese A, 'Can the Notion of Inhuman and Degrading Treatment be Applied to Socio-economic Conditions?' 2 *European Journal of International Law* (1991) 141.

Cohen J, 'Minimalism About Human Rights: the Best We Can Hope For?' 12 *Journal of Political Philosophy* (2004) 190.

Craven M, 'The Justiciability of Economic, Social and Cultural Rights' in Burchill R, Harris D, and Owers A (eds) *Economic, Social and Cultural Rights: their Implementation in UK Law* (1999) 1.

——, *The International Covenant on Economic, Social and Cultural Rights: A Perspective on its Development* (1995).

Cummiskey D, 'Kantian Consequentialism' 100 *Ethics* (1990) 586.

Darrow M and Alston P, 'Bills of Rights in Comparative Perspective' in Alston (ed) *Promoting Human Rights Through Bills of Rights* (1999) 465.

Davidson D, 'Epistemology and Truth' in Davidson D, *Subjective, Intersubjective, Objective* (2001) 177.

Davidson D, *Inquiries into Truth and Interpretation* (2001).

——, 'A Coherence Theory of Truth and Knowledge' reprinted in *Subjective, Intersubjective, Objective* (2001).

——, 'Empirical Content' in *Subjective, Intersubjective, Objective* (2001).

——, 'Belief as the basis of meaning' in *Inquiries into Truth and Interpretation*, at 153.

——, 'On the very idea of a conceptual scheme' reprinted in *Inquiries into Truth and Interpretation* (2nd edn, 2001) 183.

——, 'The folly of trying to define truth' 93 *Journal of Philosophy* (1996) 263.

——, *Subjective, Intersubjective, Objective* (2001).

——, 'Afterthoughts' to 'A Coherence Theory of Truth' in *Subjective, Intersubjective, Objective* (2001).

Davidson JS, *The Inter-American Human Rights System* (1997).

de Blois M, 'The Fundamental Freedom of the European Court of Human Rights' in Lawson R, de Blois M (eds) *The Dynamics of the Protection of Human Rights in Europe* (1994) 51.

Dembour MB, '"Finishing Off" Cases: The Radical Solution to the Problem of the Expanding ECtHR Caseload' 5 *European Human Rights Law Review* (2002) 604.

Devlin P, *The Enforcement of Morals* (1965).

Dickson J, 'Methodology in Jurisprudence: A Critical Survey' 10 *Legal Theory* (2004) 117.

Dijk V, Hoof V, *Theory and Practice of the European Convention on Human Rights* (2nd edn, 1990).

Doyle M, 'Kant, Liberal Legacies and Foreign Affairs' 12 *Philosophy and Public Affairs* (1983) 205.

Drzemczewski A, 'The European Human Rights Convention: Protocol No. 11–Entry Into Force and First Year of Application' 21 *Human Rights Law Journal* (2000) 1.

Dworkin R, 'Hard Cases' in Dworkin R, *Taking Rights Seriously* (1977).

——, 'The Model of Rules I', in Dworkin R, *Taking Rights Seriously* (1977).

——, 'Rights as Trumps' in Waldron J (ed) *Theories of Rights* (1984) 153.

——, 'The Forum of Principle' in Dworkin R, *A Matter of Principle* (1985).

——, *Life's Dominion* (1993).

——, *Freedom's Law* (1996).

——, *Law's Empire* (1986).

——, 'Objectivity and Truth' 25 *Philosophy and Public Affairs* (Spring 1996).

——, 'Comment' in Gutman A, *A Matter of Interpretation* (1997).

——, *Sovereign Virtue: The Theory and Practice of Equality* (2000).

——, 'Terror and the attack on civil liberties' 50(17) *New York Review of Books* (November 6, 2003).

——, 'Hart's Postscript and the Character of Political Philosophy' 24(1) *Oxford Journal of Legal Studies* (2004) 1.

——, 'What Are Human Rights', unpublished article, available at: <http://www.law.nyu.edu/clppt/program2003/readings/dworkin.pdf>.

——, *Justice in Robes* (2006).

Endicott T, *Vagueness in Law* (2000).

——, *Is Democracy Possible Here?* (2006).

Envine S, *Donald Davidson* (1991).

Ewing KD, 'The Implications of Wilson and Palmer' 32 *Industrial Law Journal* (2003) 1.

Fabre C, *Social Rights Under the Constitution: Government and the Decent Life* (2000).

Fallon R, 'As-Applied and Facial Challenges and Third-Party Standing' 113 *Harvard Law Review* (2000) 1321.

Ferraz OLM, *An Insurance Model for the Protection of Economic and Social Rights*, PhD thesis submitted at University College London in 2004.

Frege G, 'On Sense and Reference' in Geach P, Black M (eds) *Translations from the Philosophical Writings of Gottlob Frege* (1980).

Fox GH and Roth BR, 'Democracy and International Law' 27 *Review of International Studies* (2001) 327–52.

Franck T, 'The Emerging Right to Democratic Governance' 86 *American Journal of International Law* (1992).

Frey RG, 'Act-utilitarianism' in LaFollette H, *The Blackwell Companion to Ethical Theory* (2000).

Freeman M, *Human Rights* (2002).

Fuller L, *The Morality of Law* (1964).

Gallie W, 'Essentially Contested Concepts' 56 *Proceedings of the Aristotelian Society* (1965) 167.

Geddis A, 'You Can't Say "GOD" on the Radio: Freedom of Expression, Religious Advertisement and the Broadcast Media after Murphy v Ireland' 2 *European Human Rights Law Review* (2004) 181.

Goodman R, 'Human Rights Treaties, Invalid Reservations and State Consent' 96 *American Journal of International Law* (2002) 531.

Gray T, 'Do We Have an Unwritten Constitution?' 27 *Stanford Law Review* (1975) 703.

Greer S, 'Constitutionalizing Adjudication under the European Convention on Human Rights' 23 *Oxford Journal of Legal Studies* (2003) 405.

——, 'Protocol 14 and the Future of the European Court of Human Rights' *Public Law* (Spring 2005) 83–106.

Griffin J, 'Discrepancies Between the Best Philosophical Account of Human Rights and the International Law of Human Rights' 10 *Telos* (2001) 133.

——, 'First Steps in an Account of Human Rights' 9 *European Journal of Philosophy* (2001) 306.

Gross O and Aolain FN, 'From Discretion to Scrutiny: Revisiting the Application of the Margin of Appreciation Doctrine in the Context of Article 15 of the European Convention on Human Rights' 23 *Human Rights Quarterly* (2001) 625.

——, 'Once More unto the Breach': The Systemic Failure of Applying the European Convention on Human Rights to Entrenched Emergencies' 23 *Yale Journal of International Law* (1998) 437.

Hart HLA, 'Between Utility and Rights' in Hart HLA, *Essays in Jurisprudence and Philosophy* (1983).

Hart HLA, 'Rawls on Liberty and its Priority' in Hart HLA, *Essays in Jurisprudence and Philosophy* (1993).

——, *Law, Liberty and Morality* (1963).

——, *The Concept of Law* (1994).

Helfer L and Slaughter AM, 'Toward a Theory of Effective Supranational Adjudication' 107(2) *Yale Law Journal* (1997) 273.

Helfer L, 'Consensus, Coherence and The European Convention of Human Rights' 26 *Cornell International Law Journal* (1993) 135.

Hershovitz S (ed) *Exploring Law's Empire: The Jurisprudence of Ronald Dworkin* (2006).

Horwich P, *Truth* (1991).

Kahn JD, 'Russia's "Dictatorship of Law" and the European Court of Human Rights' 29 *Review of Central and East European Law* (2004) 1.

Koji T, 'Emerging Hierarchy in International Human Rights and Beyond. From the Perspective of Non-Derogable Rights' 12 *European Journal of International Law* (2001) 917.

Kramer M, Simmonds NE, and Steiner H, *A Debate over Rights* (1998).

Kripke S, *Wittgenstein on Rules and Private Language: an elementary exposition* (1982).

Letsas G, 'International Human Rights and the Binding Force of Interim Measures' 5 *European Human Rights Law Review* (2003) 527.

Leuprecht P, 'Innovations in the European System of Human Rights Protection: Is Enlargement Compatible with Reinforcement?' 8 *Transnational Law and Contemporary Problems* (1998) 313.

Lord Lester of Herne Hill, 'Universality Versus Subsidiarity: A Reply' 1 *European Human Rights Law Review* (1998) 73.

Lyons D, 'Constitutional Interpretation and Original Meaning' 4 *Social Philosophy and Policy* (1986) 85.

Macdonald R, 'The Margin of Appreciation' in Macdonald, Matscher, and Petzold (eds) *The European System for the Protection of Human Rights* (1993) 83.

Mahoney P, 'Judicial Activism and Judicial Self-Restraint in the European Court of Human Rights: two sides of the same coin' 11 *Human Rights Law Journal* (1990) 57.

——, 'Marvellous Richness of Diversity or Invidious Cultural Relativism' 19 *Human Rights Law Journal* (1998) 2.

Mantouvalou V, 'Work and Private Life: Sidabras and Dziautas v Lithuania' 30(4) *European Law Review* (2005) 573.

Marks S, 'Civil Liberties at the Margin: the UK Derogation and the European Court of Human Rights' 15 *Oxford Journal of Legal Studies* (1995) 69.

——, 'The European Convention on Human Rights and its "democratic society"' 66 *British Yearbook of International Law* (1995) 209.

Matscher F, 'Methods of Interpretation of the Convention' in Macdonald, Matscher, and Petzold (eds) *The European System for the Protection of Human Rights* (1993).

McHarg A, 'Reconciling Human Rights and Public Interest: Conceptual Problems and Doctrinal Uncertainty in the Jurisprudence of the European Court of Human Rights' 62 *Modern Law Review* (1999) 671.

Meckled-Garcia S and Cali B (eds) *The Legalisation of Human Rights* (2005).

Meron T, 'On a Hierarchy of International Human Rights' 80 *American Journal of International Law* (1986)1.

Mowbray A, 'Duties of Investigation Under the European Convention on Human Rights' 51 *International and Comparative Law Quarterly* (2002) 437.

——, *The Development of Positive Obligations Under the European Convention on Human Rights by the European Court of Human Rights* (Hart Publishing, 2004).

Nagel T, 'Personal Rights and Public Space' 24(2) *Philosophy and Public Affairs* (1995) 83.

——, 'The Problem of Global Justice' 33(2) *Philosophy and Public Affairs* (2005) 113.

Nino C, *The Ethics of Human Rights* (1991).

Nowlin C, 'The Protection of Morals Under the European Convention for the Protection of Human Rights and Fundamental Freedoms' 24 *Human Rights Quarterly* (2002) 264.

Nozick R, *Anarchy, State and Utopia* (1974).

Orakhelashvili A, 'Restrictive Interpretation of Human Rights Treaties in the Recent Jurisprudence of the European Court of Human Rights' 14(3) *European Journal of International Law* (2003) 529.

Ost F, 'The Original Canons of Interpretation of the European Court of Human Rights' in Delmas-Marty M (ed) *The European Convention for the Protection of Human Rights* (1991) 238.

Perry MJ, 'Interpretivism, Freedom of Expression and Equal Protection' 42 *Ohio State Law Journal* (1981) 261.

Petzold H, 'The Convention and the Principle of Subsidiarity' in Macdonald, Matscher, and Petzol (eds) *The European System for the Protection of Human Rights* (1993) 41.

Pildes R, 'Why Rights Are Not Trumps: Social Meanings, Expressive Harms, and Constitutionalism' 17 *Journal of Legal Studies* (June 1998) 725.

——, 'Dworkin's Two Conceptions of Rights' 29 *Journal of Legal Studies* (January 2000) 309.

Quine WV, *From A Logical Point of View* (1953).

——, *Word and Object* (1960).

Rawls J, *A Theory of Justice* (1999 revised edn).

——, *Justice as Fairness: A Restatement* (2001).

——, *Political Liberalism* (1993).

——, *The Law of Peoples* (1999).

Raz J, 'Professor Dworkin's Theory of Rights' XXVI *Political Studies* (1978) 123.

——, 'Two views on the nature of legal theory: A partial comparison' 4 *Legal Theory* (1998) 254.

——, *The Morality of Freedom* (1998).

Rorty R, 'Human Rights, Rationality, and Sentimentality' in Shute S, Hurley S (eds) *On Human Rights: The Oxford Amnesty Lectures 1993* (1993).

Ryssdall R, 'The Coming of Age of the European Convention of Human Rights' 18 *European Human Rights Law Review* (1996) 24.

Sadurski W, 'Judicial Review and the Protection of Constitutional Rights' 22 *Oxford Journal of Legal Studies* (2002) 275.

Scalia A, 'Common Law Courts in a Civil Law System' in Gutman A (ed) *A Matter of Interpretation* (1997).

——, 'Originalism: The Lesser Evil' 57 *University of Cincinnati Law Review* (1989).

Sen A, 'Rights and Agency' 11 *Philosophy and Public Affairs* (1982) 3–39.

Shapiro M, 'Judges as Liars' 17 *Harvard Journal of Law and Public Policy* 155.

Singh R et al, 'Is there a role for the "Margin of Appreciation" in national law after the Human Rights Act?' 1 *European Human Rights Law Review* (1999) 4.

Sohn L and Buergenthal T, *International Protection of Human Rights* (1973).

Stavropoulos N, 'Hart's semantics' in Coleman (ed) *Hart's Postscript* (2001) 59.

——, *Objectivity in Law* (1996).

——, 'Interpretivist Theories of Law' in *The Stanford Encyclopedia of Philosophy*, available at <http:// plato.stanford.edu/entries/law-interpretivist/>.

Tarksi, 'The Semantic Conception of Truth' 4 *Philosophy and Phenomenological Research* (1944).

Waldron J (ed) *Theories of Rights* (1984) 6.

——, 'Pildes on Dworkin's Theory of Rights' 29 *Journal of Legal Studies* (January 2000) 309.

——, *Law and Disagreement* (1999) 232–54.

——, 'How to Argue for a Universal Claim' 30 *Columbia Human Rights Law Review* (1999) 305–14.

——, *Nonsense on Stilts: Bentham, Burke and Marx on the Rights of Man* (1987).

——, 'The Core of the Case Against Judicial Review' 115 *Yale Law Journal* (2006) 1346.

——, *Liberal Rights: Collected Papers* 1981–1991 (1993) 210.

——, 'A Right-Based Critique of Constitutional Rights', 13 *Oxford Journal of Legal Studies* (1993) 18.

Wildhaber L, 'The European Convention on Human Rights and International Law' 56 *International and Comparative Law Quarterly* (2006) 217.

Williams B, *In the Beginning was the Deed* (2005).

Yablon CM, 'Are Judges Liars? A Wittgensteinian Critique of Law's Empire' in Patterson D (ed) *Wittgenstein and Legal Theory* (1994).

Yourow H, *The Margin of Appreciation Doctrine in the Dynamics of European Human Rights Jurisprudence* (1996).

Index

ECHR = European Convention on Human Rights
ECtHR = European Court of Human Rights